CHURCH
Matters

Passionate Pleadings
That Prepare Us for the
Future

COMPILED BY

John Davis Marshall

AND 13 OTHER MEN OF GOD

Table of Contents

—ɯɯ—

Church Matters

Passionate Pleadings That Prepare Us for the Future

John Davis Marshall

—◊—

For quite some time, I have advocated that we need to begin discussing any and all pertinent Biblical issues relative to the fellowship and development of believers. Yes, we must engage in dialogue about even the divisive issues. We can no longer enjoy the luxury, sinful luxury I might add, of avoidance.

On several occasions, I discussed with the late Dr. Clyde Muse (then serving as chairman of the National Lectureship Committee) how that I believed that we should: (1) provide a forum wherein we would recognize preachers who faithfully serve small and sometimes "off the beaten path" congregations; for they rarely receive visible and verbal accolades at the lectureships and (2) provide a forum wherein we bring together men who host dissenting understandings of certain Biblical texts and allow them to objectively present their scholarly conclusions; while receptive minds listen, ask questions, and learn. Dr. Muse wholeheartedly agreed with my observation. But God saw fit for him to transition to his eternal reward before having the necessary time to implement and accomplish such a task. Now, neither of these is being done. Therefore, it is past the time to begin the dialogue. Hopefully, **CHURCH MATTERS** will set the stage for the latter to be addressed. I do agree that this is a feeble effort, but hopefully in the future, we can more adequately address our challenging issues.

Apparently, I am not alone in my perception. The 70th Annual Churches of Christ National Lectureship [April 2014] seems to agree. For their theme, they chose "Navigating Unchartered Waters: Examining Issues, Creating Solutions." May God bless the lectureship and us to continually move the discussion positively progressively along?

God warned His people that they would always encounter relevant and renovating adversities (1 Timothy 4:1-2).

Fortunately, adequately warned and armed believers can be enabled to maintain their spiritual momentum in spite of adversities (Acts 6:7).

CHURCH MATTERS *seeks to frame a spiritual thought pattern/ process to begin/continue thinking about relevant issues that are presently and will be in the near future significantly impacting our brotherhood.*

CHURCH MATTERS *seeks to begin/continue the dialogue between and among leaders/members about those relevant and impacting issues.*

CHURCH MATTERS *seeks to cause leaders/members to position/reposition themselves to minimize evil and maximize good as our brotherhood engages these relevant and impacting issues.*

Please, allow **CHURCH MATTERS** *to transmit the passion from men of faith and ignite the flame within your heart that compels and propels you to carry the torch of spiritual renovation throughout your world.*

Now Take. Read.

James Michael Crusoe

James Michael Crusoe has been associated with churches of Christ his entire life. He was baptized into Christ at age of seven, and preached his first sermon at age twenty. He is married to Debra Dilworth, and they have three children and one grandchild.

Brother Crusoe is a 1983 graduate of Abilene Christian University, receiving a MS degree in Ministry and Evangelism. His undergraduate degree is from Wittenberg University, a BA in Sociology. He has advanced postgraduate study at John Marshall Law School; Union Presbyterian School of Christian Education; Harding School of Theology; and is presently pursuing a DMin degree from Union University in Expository Preaching.

During his thirty-six years of ministry, Brother Crusoe has served churches of Christ in Arizona, Kansas, Virginia and Tennessee. A new church plant in Memphis began in January 2013 and has grown to 100 members in just eight weeks! His ministry has been blessed with baptisms at each congregation, with an average of thirty to forty baptisms each year.

He serves as a board member on the National Lectureship Advisory Committee of Churches of Christ; board member of the National Teachers Workshop of Churches of Christ; board member of the Tennessee State Lectureship; he is the founder and President of Charis Acres, Inc.; and Grace Place Retirement Community, two 501c3 organizations that serve the community by developing a thirty-unit two-story senior citizen complex.

Brother Crusoe served as the host of a national television broadcast seen on the Word Network for nine years. That broadcast reached 60 million viewers.

He has preached the gospel in thirty-one states, and five countries outside the continental USA, including Nigeria, Liberia, Jamaica, Bermuda and the Cayman Islands.

He conducts a number of revivals and gospel meetings, and speaks regularly at national and regional Church of Christ lectureships.

CHAPTER 1

Ministerial Ethics: A Theocratic Approach

James Michael Crusoe
DMin Candidate – Union University
Minister: Cherry Rd. Church of Christ,
Memphis, TN

—⟋⟋⟍—

Let's take a journey together. We might want to fasten our seat belts...for we will not always be on cruise control...there will be bumps in the road...WARNINNG SIGNS ALONG THE WAY...Yield Not to Temptation signs...CAUTION: FOR DANGER LIE AHEAD signs. We may encounter bumps in the road along the way...we may even see a Slippery When Wet sign along the way. Watch for Black Ice, which can be difficult to see but makes conditions slippery when pavement temperatures are below freezing. We should have a cell phone handy, if possible, but not text while driving; distracted driving is illegal and becomes even more dangerous during storms. We need to equip your car with emergency supplies including sand, a shovel, flares, booster cables, rope, ice scraper, portable radio, flashlight, blankets and extra warm clothes. We should inform a responsible person of our destination, intended route, and estimated time of arrival; keep calm and not panic in case of a vehicle breakdown, accident, or if we become snowbound.

The prophet Jeremiah cried "Is there no balm in Gilead, is there no physician there? Why then is not the health of the daughter of my people recovered?" What happens when the physician is in need of medical attention? Is it possible to treat the patient while neglecting our own spiritual condition? There must be a check up from the neck up. A critical self-examination will reveal that ministers of the gospel often are wounded warriors, forced to serve a fractured fellowship that is disenfranchised, discouraged and disappointed. We have a Divine pattern before us; we have medicine that has proven to bring healing, yet the mortality rate in the church continues to rise.

"Ethics" are necessary in all walks of life. Doctors take the Hippocratic Oath. Lawyers, after passing the bar exam, take an oath of office. Even barbers and lawn care specialists see the need for a code of conduct in their profession. What is ethics? It is a set of moral principles. Ethics is the discipline dealing with what is good and what is bad: moral duty and obligation. Ethics is that branch of philosophy dealing with values relating to human conduct, **with respect to the right and wrong of certain actions and the good and bad of the motives and ends of such actions.** Ethics defines **the rules of conduct recognized in respect to a particular group or culture, such as** *medical ethics or Christian ethics.* We get the word "etiquette" from the word "ethics." Joseph Earl Bush-Gentle wrote in *Shepherding: Pastoral Ethics and Leadership*: "Ethics become important as people make decisions that affect other people and as they participate in lifestyles that affect future generations or for the earth as a whole." It is important to keep in mind that we also model behavior by our ethics.

This chapter invites the reader to take a journey toward a theocratic approach to ethics in the ministry. By theocratic, I simply mean developing an ethical mind-set modeled after the creative work of the Triune God. Even though the Fall corrupted humanity's morals, kingdom living is an attempt to restore what was lost in the Garden of Eden. The chapter will begins with a theocratic perspective, followed by a historical perspective and concluded with practical suggestions.

Ministerial Ethics: The Triune Godhead Model

Genesis 1: 26 Then God said, "Let Us make man in Our image, according to Our likeness; and let them rule over the fish of the sea and over the birds of the sky and over the cattle and over all the earth, and over every creeping thing that creeps on the earth." 27 God created man in His own image, in the image of God He created him; male and female He created them. (NASB)

The first man was created in the very image and likeness of God. Divinity took dust, shaped dust and breathed into dust the breath of life, and then dust became a living soul. There was a divine connection between God and man. God breathed something into man. The breath of God was holy, pure, spiritual and good. What does that gift mean to us today?

Perhaps an understanding of breath will help. Breath and spirit are sometimes identical in ancient languages. In Latin, it means to "aspire, conspire, inspire, perspire and expire." In Greek, it means "pneumatic and pneumonia." One word refers to any tool that is air operated; the second word refers to a disease of lungs or the breath box. In Hebrew, there is a word that has the sound of breath, like wind. God breathed some of Himself into His creation. Breath for us is life. Breath for us is movement and activity. The first man had a special relationship to God by virtue of God's breath inside him.

We are reminded in scripture to be holy, as God is holy. A holy God is an ethical God.

The bar was raised when Divinity breathed the breath of life into dust, but sadly, since the Fall, humanity has fallen short of God's original intent. We now dwell in a valley of dry bones of pseudospiritual and pseudomoral values that hinder the growth of the Kingdom of God. We find ourselves living in a culture that is comfortable with wrong being right and right being wrong. New sets of rules dominate. Sadly, those rules are distorted and warped.

A sin nature began in the Fall, thus affecting our character, which in turns becomes a matter of ethics. If truth were told, since the Fall, there has been an ethical dilemma. Humanity no longer is connected spiritually to the Creator—God. We now find ourselves broken, separated, and lost.

A story is told of Henry Ward Beecher that reminds us of the cut that sin caused in the Garden of Eden. In 1872, Henry Ward Beecher traveled to Yale to deliver the first of the Beecher Lectures on preaching. He had experienced a bad night, not feeling well. He went to his hotel, got his dinner, and lay down to take a nap. About 2:00 a.m., he got up and began to shave. Up to that point, he had not planned the lecture to be delivered within the hour. Just as he had his face lathered and was beginning to strop his razor, the whole idea came out of nowhere and dawned on him. Beecher cut himself with his razor and wrote out notes for the first Beecher lectures in blood, because whatever he aspired to be, or was famous for being, he was a man of flesh and blood. Beecher saw two images in the mirror: the man he wanted to be and the person he had become. That is the core of ethics—who we are versus who we are trying to be.

SOMETIMES WE CUT OURSELVES BADLY

Sometimes there are cracks in the ministerial mirror. Sometimes those cracks break under pressure. In a sermon on ministerial ethics, Dr. Jerry Taylor spoke about "a fault line" that causes earthquakes. These fault lines are under the ground, but leave holes above ground. Every human being has "faults" or "cracks." Those faults or cracks come in the form of greed, lust and power. Every preacher has to face these deadly three: greed, lust, and power. Who we are is determined by how we respond to pressure when faced with the "fault lines" of life.

Ideally, we should contain our selfish pride and enormous ego; however the dilemma of reality is that we often are consumed with self. What we want, where we want to be, and how many do we have following us become the driving force. Ministry, the pulpit, and congregations are used as pedestals to perpetuate a self-induced fantasy that God needs us more than we need God.

Whatever happened to character, integrity and honesty? It has been suggested that character plus conduct equal integrity. A key aspect of ethics is honesty. It is my conviction that one may not always be right in thoughts and actions, but we should always be honest about our thoughts and actions. The difference is between "being" and "doing." I want to suggest that "who we are" determines "what we do." How often do we define ourselves by what we do to describe who we are? I am a Christian who preaches for a living. What I do is closely related to who I am; so close that they are inseparable. What the minister is will be his greatest sermon, but we must keep in mind that what a minister does is sometimes not nearly as important as what a minister is. We do not just perform a ministry; we are Christians first who serve by preaching. This is a paradox that was understood by Augustine's statement, "For you I am a bishop but with you I am a Christian." Aristotle believed that good works arise from good people, and in order to do good, one must gain wisdom, experience and self-control.

God the Father, Jesus the Son, and the Holy Spirit, who is the Comforter, are the embodiment of integrity. Perry Shaw wrote, "Central to the biblical account of Creation are two key teachings: (a) the fiat creative work of God—the Triune God commands

13

and it is—and it is good, and (b) the Creation of humans in the image of God." There was a Trinitarian action of teamwork, cooperation and delegation. Each played a crucial role. The Father did not create without the Son, nor was the Spirit excluded. Integrity is a combination of ethics, character and morals. The members of the Godhead possess integrity because of their Divine nature. Henry Cloud said, "Who a person is will ultimately determine if their [sic] brain, talents, energy and opportunities will succeed." Integrity is about being a whole person, an integrated person. Ethics in ministry takes place when all of our different parts work together and deliver the functions they were designed to deliver.

Ministerial Ethics: A Historical Perspective

H. Richard Niebuhr called the ministry of his generation, "a perplexed profession." Indeed, it is, but part of the problem is how one views the ministry. Some see the ministry as a career or a calling…an occupation or a vocation…is a minister a professional or one who professes by a higher standard of living? In a contemporary context, a professional is "a broadly educated person of highly developed skills and knowledge, primarily concerned with the interests of the community rather than his own."

The word "profess" originally meant "to testify on behalf of or to stand for something." Originally, the term "professional" was applied to members of the clergy. A professional was first a person who had something to profess, some body of knowledge, in allegiance to some notion of the higher good, some attachment to goals more significant than self. The professional was a person who knew something that benefited the wider community and had the responsibility to use that knowledge to serve the wider community. Being a professional meant one was a person of knowledge and responsibility. What we profess to be defines our fundamental commitment to the community.

In early Israel, a special class of religious professionals developed: the prophets and priests. They were the authority in law and religion. That's why prophets like Amos would preach against dishonest and unethical business practices. That's why Ezekiel's charge in Ezekiel 22 is so harsh. It was the prophets, priests, and princes who were unethical in their dealings.

By the time of Jesus, a variety of professions had emerged: priests, teachers, lawyers, physicians and even professional soldiers. During the middle ages, the clergy became the dominant professional group. They controlled education and wrote the rules governing the practice of other professions. During the Reformation period, the professions stagnated, became small and exclusive. Members of the profession led the "good life," gaining high social status through attachment to the King. During this period, the major professions were medicine, law, and the clergy. The pastor would also be judge, doctor, lawyer, magistrate and teacher.

I believe the best approach that moves us closer to a theocratic ethic is to view ministry as a vocation and calling. Notice what took place in the call of the prophet Isaiah. In the presence of God, Isaiah recognized that he was unclean and unholy. There was a purging and restoration before a call and commitment to serve. (Isaiah 6:1-8) It is undeniable that a call to ministry is a matter of Grace. The Spirit of God gives birth to the call, the Spirit births us, forms us, helps us, empowers us, and equips us for service. The call may take place before birth as it did with Jeremiah, or it may be a Damascus road experience, or without reservation, responding to a "follow me" statement. Regardless, it leaves the ethical minister with the sense of this responsibility: "Woe is me if I preach not the gospel of Christ."

Ministerial Ethics: Not Autocratic or Democratic

Perry Shaw stated, "Throughout the Scriptures the ideal model is not that of democracy or autocracy but theocracy; leaders see themselves as, first and foremost, servants and followers under the authority and leadership of God." He continues by saying, "As Christianity becomes an increasingly global phenomenon, it is imperative for Christian leaders to examine cultural factors in leadership theology." We must honestly admit that when it comes to ministerial ethics, cultural patterns reflect images of the Divine nature and images of the Fall. The following are some incorrect, and in my opinion, unethical approaches to ministerial ethics.

INCORRECT MODELS

- **SPIRITUAL CEO**...<u>ACTIVE IS THE OPERATIVE WORD FOR THIS STYLE</u>
1. THIS LEADER MAKES THINGS HAPPEN NO MATTER WHAT IT TAKES
2. RATHER THAN DOING MINISTRY, HE DIRECTS MINISTRY LIKE AN EXECUTIVE OR DIRECTOR
  " PREACHERS WHO SEE THEMSELVES AS CEO'S AND OPERATE THEIR CHURCHES LIKE LARGE CORPORATIONS SEEM TO HAVE FORGOTTEN THEY WERE CALLED BY GOD TO BE SERVANTS"

- **POLITICAL DICTATOR**...<u>AUTHORITATIVE IS THE OPERATIVE WORD</u>...THEY MAKE THEIR WILL KNOWN AND EXPECT IT TO BE CARRIED OUT

- **"HIRED HAND MODEL"**...<u>THE OPERATIVE WORD IS PASSIVE</u>...THEY SIMPLY DO WHAT THEY ARE TOLD AND GO WHERE THEY ARE DIRECTED

BEST MODEL: THEOCRATIC

- **SERVANT MODEL**...<u>RESPONSIVE IS THE BETTER MODEL</u>...THE MINISTER WHO IS A SERVANT RESPONDS TO THE NEEDS OF THE PEOPLE, RESPONDS TO THE DIRECTIVES OF GOD, AND RESPONDS TO THE GUIDANCE OF THE HOLY SPIRIT

Joseph E. Bush in the book, *Gentle Shepherding: Pastoral Ethics and Leadership*, shares suggestions to bring us closer to ethical leadership in ministry.

LEADERSHIP DEALS WITH DIRECTION
MANAGEMENT DEALS WITH SPEED

LEADERSHIP DEALS WITH VISION
MANAGEMENT DEALS WITH STRUCTURE AND SYSTEMS

LEADERSHIP FOCUSES ON THE TOP LINE
MANAGEMENT FOCUSES ON THE BOTTOM LINE

LEADERSHIP IS CONCERNED ABOUT VALUES AND CORRECT PRINCIPLES
MANAGEMENT ORGANIZES RESOURCES

Ministerial Ethics: A Practical Theocratic Approach

Matthew 6: 9-10 9 "Pray, then, in this way: 'Our Father who is in heaven, Hallowed be Your name. 10 Your kingdom come. Your will be done, On earth as it is in heaven. (NASB)

For the most part, the body of Christ is often in a dysfunctional state. How can we teach unity in the body when those who lead do not practice what we preach? It is difficult to remove a cancer when we contribute to spreading of the disease. Ethics is "thrown out the window if the price is right." Again, I appeal to a theocratic model of ministry: God, the Son, did not betray the Father; the Spirit of God was cooperative with Jesus, the Son.

The spiritual connection was corrupted in the Garden. When sin entered, man became broken, separated, fractured and fallen. It is important to understand this concept because it is the core of who we are and why we do what we do. I maintain that one cannot fully comprehend the ethical dilemma until one looks at the three

Ws in life. The three Ws are "who, what and why." These determine the core being of a person.

Kingdom living forces the "brotherhood" to avoid being "brothers in the hood" who are more "hood" than "brothers." Ministers share the same grief, the same struggles, the same trials and temptations. We may handle them differently, but the truth is, that we are all "in this thing together." The key is to continue to look to the Godhead as the example. The model prayer in the gospel of Matthews says, "God's will is to be done on earth as His will is in heaven." The Father, Son and Holy Spirit were ethical in Creation, Redemption and Salvation. There is no jealousy, no competition, no dishonesty, and no showmanship, between the Godhead Three.

How sad that we limit the kingdom to just being the church without emphasizing the reign and rule of God in the "life of the believer." Preachers were Christians before they became ministers. We are to demonstrate the fruits of the Spirit as well as anyone else. There are no special rules for us that do not apply across the board.

Charles Tupper authored a book, *Called In Honor*. He has a chapter entitled, "Preachers, Help Each Other." He states, "There is a natural affinity between men of similar education, of like pastorates, and of mutually congenial theology...and these common experiences often become the basis for cliques in which there is a fertile field for caustic criticism of others. Jealousy and envy may seize even the elect...discourtesy in the common amenities of good manners may be exhibited. Thus a fellowship which should be ideal has the capacity to deteriorate into something highly undesirable." It cannot be avoided; we have to face the issue of ministers being colleagues rather than competitors. I mentioned earlier in the chapter that barbers and lawn care specialists have ethics in their respective professions. My barber stated that he will not take another barbers customer, and a brother I know who cuts grass stated that he does not go after a competitor's lawn.

We must be careful to avoid taking a legalistic, ritualistic approach. Stanley Hauerwas wrote, "The temptation is to think the task to be the development of a code, similar to that of the medical and legal professions, to guide the training and/or behavior of ministers." I have no wish to deny the usefulness of such codes or to deny that such a code might be of some use for the ministry. However, I think that such a "legalistic" response would be insufficient for helping us develop a sense of the kind of morality appropriate to the ministry. For in the ministry, as well as the law and medicine, involves more than questions of what is permissible and not permissible, but raises the question of the kind of persons that we should be as ministers. It is not enough, in other words, that those called to the ministry refrain from, or do certain things, but it is necessary that they be the kind of persons, who have the character to sustain them in the ministry.

PRACTICAL POINTS

1 Timothy 4:1-6 But the Spirit explicitly says that in later times some will fall away from the faith, paying attention to deceitful spirits and doctrines of demons, 2 by means of the hypocrisy of liars seared in their own conscience as with a branding iron, 3 *men* who forbid marriage *and advocate* abstaining from foods which God has created to be gratefully shared in by those who believe and know the truth. 4 For everything created by God is good, and nothing is to be rejected if it is received with gratitude; 5 for it is sanctified by means of the word of God and prayer. 6 In pointing out these things to the brethren, you will be a good servant of Christ Jesus, *constantly* nourished on the words of the faith and of the sound doctrine which you have been following. (NASB)

In order to be good ministers in a not so good world, the ethical minister must understand himself. Reinhold Niebuhr reminded us that human nature has the capacity for self-deception, accepting evil in the guise of good. An ethical minister is one who is honorable and can be trusted to do what is right. An ethical minister is not like:

- Cain who could not be trusted to rule over the desire of envy and jealousy and killed his brother

- Nadab and Abihu, who could not be trusted to offer the fire that God commanded

- The sons of Eli, who could not be trusted with the women that assembled at the door of the Tabernacle

- Like Judas, who carried the bag, but sold his soul for 30 pieces of silver

There are a number of ethical examples in scripture. We need more:

- Saints like Daniel who would rather face the Lion's Den than pray in secret

- Men like Joseph who can be trusted to leave their coats and run, instead of taking advantage of a stolen moment

- Leaders like Moses who chose to suffer affliction rather than enjoy the pleasures of sin for a season

THE PREDECESSOR AND SUCCESSOR

What is your relationship to your successor when you are the predecessor? The minister should communicate clearly if and when the mantle will be passed. It is neither fair nor healthy for the congregation or the new minister to hold on to the reigns indefinitely. Nolan B. Harmon stated, "Above all when a man leaves a charge, let him leave. No minister should be constantly going back to gossip with the brethren or hear comments on the work of his successor." It is ethical for a former minister when asked to perform a wedding or funeral to go through the present minister.

It is ethical to assist the present minister, but allow the present minister to function as the minister.

The successor should study the plans and goals of the predecessor. If possible, attempt to communicate with the predecessor as a matter of courtesy.

1. MINISTERS & ASSISTANTS...

The assistant should be careful not to get caught up in the accolades of the members. Be careful not to let the compliments "swell your head." Joshua was the servant of Moses, and Elisha was the servant of Elijah. Ethics demand speaking well of the minister. When there is a transition over a period of time, the new minister must always speak well of the former minister. This ideal is true even after the departure of the former minister. Beware of the "Bermuda Triangle" that can take place. Members can get you to "a place of no return" by making false accusations about the former minister. But the new minister must always speak well of the former preacher. It was my practice to allow the former minister to keep his office, to offer him regular preaching opportunities, and to share the annual love offering that was given to the minister of the church.

2. THE MINISTER AND OTHER CONGREGATIONS

Under no circumstances should a minister seek to "steal sheep" from another congregation. We are in the business of "feeding" sheep not corralling members from other churches of Christ.

3. THE MINISTER AND OTHER MINISTERS

There should be camaraderie among ministers. A true brotherhood should exist, instead of the mentality that the ministry consists of a "hood of brothers." Sadly, ministers are viewed as "a dime a dozen," and expendable. "No man is an island, isolated to himself." If there is any empathy in the ministry, it should be provided by a fellow minister. It is unethical to manipulate, sabotage or undermine another man's ministry in order to take that minister's job. There are just some situations the ethical minister will avoid.

The relationship that ministers have toward other ministers is an ethical issue. It is true, "No man is an island, entire of itself; every man is a piece of the continent, a part of the main." Samuel Pounds, who preaches in Winter Haven, Florida is a preacher's preacher and a true friend of mine; has made some strong points of true friendship. He stated in a sermon that a true friend will restore you—Galatians 6:1-2, confront you—Galatians 2:11-14; and encourage you—Acts 11:22. It's not only the moral issues of fidelity, and vices that threaten our salvation. The way we model becomes a matter of ethics. Bad behavior between ministers teaches the church to treat each other the same way and contributes to the lack of respect that members have for the honorable and holy calling of ministry.

It's sad that in the "preaching business" there is a problem of greed, lust, and envy in the pulpit. While we are accountable to God, ministers are also accountable to one another. Paul did confront Peter to his face. I'm glad that Paul was not seeking Peter's pulpit, but concerned about Peter's soul. The lure of more money, higher visibility, and a bigger church have caused friends to become foes. We overlook the minister's wife and family. It's one thing to be mistreated by those who sit in the pew. It's disheartening, to say the least, when negative treatment or antagonistic behavior comes from fellow ministers. The temptation is great, and in the end it is not worth the damage that it causes.

4. CHURCH PLANTING

The motivation for a church plant is an ethical decision. Far too often, churches are planted for the wrong reason. How often do we hear of conflict and discontent being the reason that a new work begins? Church splits hurt all parties involved, divide families and leave a stain on the reputation of the church in the community. We should be careful to plant a church based on the right motivation. One motivation ought to be that the call of God was on the minister's heart to help a group after a church split.

The primary reason for planting a church, of course, is the need for a church in the community. Hozell Francis wrote in *Church Planting in the African-American Context*, "A sincere desire to reach a given "target group" with the gospel message and to disciple that group is [sic]of utmost importance in church planting. The emphasis is not on the servant but on the quality of the service." I believe that the call of God ought to be on a preacher that supersedes his personal desires. A lack of ministerial ethics causes ministers to plant a church just because they desire a place to preach. J. S. Winston, a deceased pioneer preacher in churches of Christ, prophetically stated, "You don't find a church for a preacher, but you find a preacher for a church." Winston meant that it takes the right person for the right job.

HOW DO WE HANDLE PROFESSIONAL DISTANCE?

Professional distance does not mean indifference, but that there should be a balance of empathy and objectivity. Ministers must show unconditional love and identify with people and at the same time, separate from their inner turmoil to sustain objective judgment. Ethics suggest that a good minister will take precautions to avoid potentially destructive sexual dynamics that could occur.

CONFIDENTIALITY

There are some issues that a minister has an ethical responsibility to make public. Crimes such as child abuse, sex offences, murder, assaults, robbery or even a potential suicide, cannot be held in confidence. It should be made clear that a criminal offense is not a lawyer/client privilege. In a church setting, the leadership team can be appraised in a general way in many circumstances. We are concerned with eternal matters.

GRIEF COUNSELING

How do you handle a member who is unaware of a terminal illness asking, "am I dying," or "do I have long to live?" Ministers must demonstrate effective counseling skills.

FIDELITY IN PREACHING

There is an ethic in preaching, just as there is an ethic in scholarly research. The ultimate end is that knowledge and data cannot be fudged. There are a number of things to avoid: plagiarism, copyright violation, slander, and libel. Serious study of the Word of God must be a priority. A minister has an ethical charge to uphold the doctrines and generally accepted in churches of Christ. It's a matter of respect as well as biblical integrity to honor practices that do not shipwreck the faith of others.

CONCLUSION

Of course there are a number of areas that could be addressed: finances, family, accountability, and personal growth and development. An ethical minister will take heed of the doctrine that he teaches. An ethical minister will take heed of the manner he builds on another man's foundation. An ethical minister will attempt to embody the example of the members of the Godhead in daily ministry.

Ethics in ministry is really about practicing "good shepherding skills." I use the term "shepherd" for all in ministry who care for the flock, whether it be preaching, teaching, counseling, mentoring or modeling behavior. Ministers are shepherds in the sense that we guard, protect, feed, care for and nurture those we minister to. Sheep ought to be led by trustworthy, honest, Christ-centered leaders who are aware of their humanity, yet sincerely striving to conform to the image of Divinity.

Ethics is about being a whole person; being aware of what really drives the minister who has the privilege of serving the flock of God. What we do cannot be separated from who we are. If ministers ignore or fail to submit to an ethical standard in ministry, the sheep will suffer. In the words of the prophet Jeremiah, "the harvest is past, the summer is ended, and we are not saved."

RESOURCES

Bush, Joseph E. *Gentle Shepherding: Pastoral Ethics and Leadership*. Chalice Press, St. Louis, Missouri, 2006.

Cloud, Henry. *Integrity: The Courage To Meet The Demands of Reality.* HarperCollins Publishers. New York, 2006.

Integrity—more than simple honesty, it's the key to success. A person with integrity has the ability to pull everything together, to make it all happen no matter how challenging the circumstances. Drawing on experiences from his work, Dr. Henry Cloud, a clinical psychologist, leadership coach, corporate consultant and nationally syndicated radio host, shows how our character can keep us from achieving all we want to (or could) be.

Gula, Richard. *Ethics In Pastoral Ministry*. Paulist Press, Mahwah, N.J., 1996.

In a conversational style the author offers a theological ethical framework for reflecting on the moral demands that arise from the professional exercise of the pastoral ministry.

Harmon, Nolan B. *Ministerial Ethics and Etiquette.* Abingdon Press, Nashville, 1998.

A classic guide to **ethics** since 1928. Nolan Harmon studied the ethical codes of conduct of five major denominations and secured the opinions of eighty-six leading pastors. Harmon uses this wisdom to show ministers how to conduct themselves ethically in virtually every situation.

Francis, Hozell C. *Church Planting In The African-American Context*. Grand Rapids: Zondervan, 1999.

Milco, Michael R. *Ethical Dilemmas In Church Leadership: Case Studies in Biblical Decision Making.* Kregal Publications, Grand Rapids, Michigan, 1997.

Child abuse, AIDS, infidelity, homosexuality, unexpected pregnancies. **Mike Milco** shares case studies on some of the most sensitive issues pastors and church leaders may have to deal with. Child abuse, AIDS, infidelity, homosexuality, unexpected pregnancies.

Noyce, Gaylord. *Pastoral Ethics: Professional Responsibilities of the Clergy.* Abingdon Press, Nashville, 1998.

Like most community leaders, clergy are constantly asked to make decisions that have far-reaching effects. For clergy, the matter is particularly complicated because of the many arenas in which they operate—counseling, church management, community affairs, ecumenical relationships, denominational politics, and others.

Shaw, Perry W. H. "Vulnerable Authority: A Theological Approach to Leadership and Teamwork." Christian Education Journal. Series 3, Vol. 3 ,No. 1, 2006.

Sibley, Tom. "The Preachers Challenge: To Walk the Talk."
- Evangelical Journal of Theology / Vol. 1, No. 1 (2007), pp. 107-115.

This essay affirms that clergy ethics is the resultant life and personal activity, which are derived from a transformed character, developed and shaped by faithful obedience to the practical instruction concerning relational responsibilities found in the teachings of Jesus.

Trull, Joe E. and James E. Carter. *Ministerial Ethics: Moral Formation For Church Leaders.* Baker Academic, Grand Rapids, MI, 2004.

Ministerial Ethics provides both new and experienced pastors with tools for sharpening their personal and professional decision-making skills. The authors seek to explain the unique moral role of the minister and the ethical responsibilities of the vocation.

Tupper, Charles E. *Called-In Honor.* Bethany Press, St. Louis, Missouri, 1949.

Wiest, Walter E. and Elwyn A. Smith. *Ethics In Ministry: A Guide For The Professional.* Fortress Press, Minneapolis, 1990.

An ethical guide for clergy and laypersons who deal with" the vexing questions that arise in the daily life of a minister at work." The authors discuss salaries, truth-telling, surviving church politics, confidentiality, the unmarried pastor, the two-clergy family, accepting gifts.

Willimon, William H. *Calling and Character: Virtues of the Ordained Life.* Abingdon Press, Nashville, 2000.

In Calling & Character, Willimon lays out a clear and compelling picture of the pastoral life, one that will inform both those embarking on ordained ministry and those who have been in it for many years. He lays out specific habits such as study, collegiality, and humor as the day-by-day means of following the difficult and dangerous, yet deeply rewarding, calling of a pastor.

MINISTERIAL ETHICS By I. Parker Maxey
A Guide to Ministerial Ethics and Etiquette
"That The Ministry Be Not Blamed" (2 Cor. 6:3)
ISBN 0-88019-222-4
Schmul Publishing Co., Inc.
Wesleyan Book Club 1987
Salem, Ohio

Michael L. Dublin Sr.

Michael L. Dublin Sr. has provided pastoral leadership for South Central church of Christ in Raleigh for almost thirty years. He began his journey in ministry at Brooks Ave church of Christ in Raleigh as an interim minister before moving to Rochester Heights church of Christ (now South Central church of Christ).

The congregation has grown in maturity and numbers through the blessings of God on several ministries including substance abuse training, foster care and adoption, youth, young adult, women, men and technology among many others.

He has also served professionally as an Internationally Certified Substance Abuse Prevention Specialist for the past twenty eight years while providing local and national training.

He coordinates Faith Works Together, an initiative supported by the NC Dept. of Health and Human Services.

He has been married to Cecelia Crim of Dayton, Ohio for over twenty-eight years and is still overwhelmed by her love for God as displayed daily. They have a cherished blended family of two sons, four daughters, thirteen grandchildren and four great grandchildren.

Michael earned a BA in Liberal Studies from Shaw University, Raleigh, NC and a MA in Liberal Studies from Duke University, Durham, NC

CHAPTER 2

Beyond the Borders:
The Community Matters

Michael L. Dublin Sr.

—⚬⚬—

"For God so loved the world that He gave His one and only Son that whoever believed in Him would not perish but have eternal life. For God did not send His son into the world to condemn the world, but to save the world through Him (John 3:16-17, NIV)

"Jesus went through all the towns and villages teaching in their synagogues, preaching the good news of the kingdom and healing every disease and sickness. When He saw the crowds He had compassion on them, because they were like sheep without a shepherd. Then He said to His disciples "the harvest is plentiful but the workers are few. Ask the Lord of the harvest to send out workers into the harvest field" (Matthew 9:35-38, NIV)

"Then the angel showed me the river of the water of life flowing from the throne of God and of the Lamb down the middle of the great street of the city. On each side of the river stood the tree of life, bearing twelve crops of fruit, yielding its fruit every month. And the leaves of the tree are for the healing of the nations" (Revelation 22:1-2, NIV)

The three passages alone express the will of God for the world to be saved and to be healed as a part of salvation. Baptism is not the only goal, but rather a life where people are no longer wandering in search of life and being discouraged, lead astray, and without hope. Clearly, Jesus came to the earth to restore the love God had and has for His creation.

Somehow, too many of His disciples have allowed that core Christ mission to elude them over the years. For reasons too complex for this article, the church has often isolated itself from the world and lost sight of the heart of the message of God that He loves the world and knows their situation. He has fulfilled His promise of redemption through Jesus Christ, His son for all who would believe. However, before the church can increase its relevancy in each community, each congregation must assess its own internal spiritual health.

Of course, a congregation is made up of individuals: some married, single, divorced, dating, children, youth, young adults and elderly, likely with different backgrounds, class status, ethnicities, political, educational, and myriad views of Christianity. Each congregation is held together by the love of God for them manifested in the life, death, resurrection and ascendency to the Father by Jesus Christ.

The sins of each are covered by the blood of Jesus and the love of God opens life such that the congregation can thrive as a community held together by God, Himself. Such a community depends on the revealed Word of God that is written in the sixty-six books of the Bible.

This same community is a manifestation of the work of the Holy Spirit who is the Gift that guides the community in truth. Although interpreted, misinterpreted, used and misused, it contains the holy Word, the Bible that creates transformation in the church community when applied through service to others, who have a willing servants heart and mind that is put to action without compulsion. Who is ready at a moment's notice to pray, cook, visit, listen, share financially or however one is needed in the church community?

Is I Corinthians chapter 13 a reality? Jesus said, "A new command I give you, love one another." First John expands on love in such breadth and depth that one wonders if it is contained in each member's Bible. When a congregation seeks to grow in love, it can't help but remember that is was as the song writer stated "Love Lifted Me" (James Rowe).

We fall into the pit of forgetfulness too often and can't figure out why society is as it is. We are reminded that "we too were once among them." A spirituality healthy congregation thrives because each person knows they were lost and separated from God until hearing the good news of Jesus and His offer of salvation through acceptance of Him as the only One who could and would save us. Equally important is the awareness that this salvation is offered free to everyone who hears the good news and accepts it. However, Christians must share this salvation message in the most personal way possible and as often as possible.

To have a hope in this life and the life to come, the church must take seriously the expectation of Christ Jesus that we will be the "salt of the earth" and "light of the world." Are we thriving as a people who have been captives to sin, but are now "set free"? Are we truly "new creations" (II Cor. 5:17)? How could those who are salt, light and new not be attracting others who are dying by the moment? When the church community views society as the enemy to be shunned and feared at all cost, how can we be in line with our core mission to make disciples (Matthew 28:19-20)?

How does a Christian community face the same issues of life as the surrounding society, yet look to a hope that sustains life? How does a Christian handle the untimely death of a two-year-old through accidental drowning? How does a Christian handle divorce, financial loss, addiction in the family, as well as the uncertainty all people experience?

How do Christians look beyond society's false hope, presented in the form of purchasing items that are supposed to give happiness and a sense of well-being? Are Christians shopping on Thanksgiving and Christmas for the sake of saving a few dollars, yet without giving any reflective thought to sacredness? It does not matter that these holidays are not in scripture as much as the idea that God's redeemed offer no hope any different than the malls! Where can the shopped out, left out, material weary find hope if the church is closed for the holiday to shop? Where is the salt, light, hope for the world? Where are "transformed by the renewing of your mind" Christians who engage the society out of a newness that is in awe of God and seeks to worship Him with reverence rather than a brief assembly on Sunday morning?

Church buildings remain empty during the summer as the finances needed to do God's work follow the vacations, reunions, cruises, etc. In and of themselves, there is nothing ungodly about these things except when they become more important than God and the society that is dying while some churches struggle to keep the doors open! "For Christ's love compels us, because we are convinced that One died for all, and therefore all died, and He died for all, that those who live should no longer live for themselves but for Him who died for them and was raised again" (II Corinthians 5:14-15).

A church driven by Christ will by its very nature go into society to tell the good news, the gospel of the love of God that brings joy, peace, comfort, hope and love in the midst of sorrow, suffering and hopelessness.

Small congregations may think they are too small to reach out. Once again Jesus said "For where two or three come together in my name, there am I with them" (Matthew 18:20). Yes, without God any congregation can say numbers and limited resources are the key reason for not engaging the society with a message from God. However, any church with a God-directed vision for the local community knows there is a starting point from which God will launch His outreach, His mission. What is at the heart of that small group? Why do some feed the homeless, some lead addicts to recovery, some are healing places for the divorced, some have a heart for those incarcerated, some focus on children and youth while others find community partnerships to address foster care and adoption, after school and weekend academic academies?

Surely, this is only a very small set of examples, but the point is, if you have the heart of God and seek Him through concentrated prayer, He will direct your path. "The harvest is plentiful" you will not have to sit around without a mission being fulfilled!

When Christians know their mission, they are not bound by fears of sagging pants, swagging, dread locked hair, purple spiked hair or any of the rebelliousness of youth and young adults. We remember that the fashion is often a façade masking hopelessness and fears of life. The loud and rude youth are often vying for attention, needing to be accepted!

Has the church forgotten "Just as I am"? And rewritten it to "Just as we want you to be "? Are there any "good Samaritans" or just good readers of the story Jesus told to make a point that is often missed 2000 years later?

Would Anyone Notice your Congregation's Departure? How relevant is your congregation to the community that it is best positioned to serve geographically? Many congregations have a large percentage of members driving to the assemblies from communities outside of the location of the building and may not have any sense of attachment or mission to the residents surrounding the building.

Why not plan to be of interest to the community in which the congregation worships? If the mission statement from Jesus is "go ye and make disciples," why not start in one's own backyard or across the street?

If after prayerfully seeking the path God will open for community engagement, the congregation must look at the leadership's capacity to set a vision and maintain an eye on that vision at all times. Matured leadership recognizes its strengths and weaknesses and seeks help in planning and implementing a strategic plan with faith that God has already prepared the way.

The first step in that strategic plan is to find out what the community needs that the congregation can supply or assist with finding the resources for the identified need. Does the local after school youth serving agency have space to provide education and life skills training? Does the local school need volunteers in a variety of capacities that the congregation can provide? Is there a need for drug prevention programs that involve both the youth and their parents or guardians? Is English as a second language a primary need for the Latino/Hispanic population?

The second step is to determine what the resources are and what resources will be needed to address the identified issue. That includes finances and human resources as well as books, computer access, transportation, food, language interpreters, qualified professionals, paraprofessionals, and nonprofessionals.

The third step involves planning. Planning may involve research on model programs used by churches or other faith-based organizations. If no models exist for the efforts that are being addressed, the plan must look at the overall thrust of what this effort hopes to produce. Questions, like as a result of this effort what specifically will happen? Will the target population develop a more favorable attitude towards education? Will they have a less favorable attitude towards drug use? Will families have better communication skills? Will five residents learn to speak English proficiently?

The fourth step involves actual implementation of the plan. Role delineation is crucial to ensure that implementation gets off to a good start. When roles and responsibilities are clarified, the chances for a successful outcome increase. If there are collaborative partners, the individual and corporate communities need to have clear communication mechanisms in place or the capacity to do so as unseen problems arise as is inevitable.

The fifth step, evaluation, is critical to the entire process. What did we plan to do? Did we do it? How did we do it? What did not happen as planned? What needs to be given more time and attention? What was the result, the outcome? Evaluation is not scary, but an important part of Jesus' admonition to "count the cost."

Community Collaboration

Often, churches have a "go it alone" mind-set for myriad reasons including who will get credit for the work. I believe the primary reason based on working with faith and community partnerships for twenty years is fear. Churches and other faith-based organizations are fearful of each other because of the differences in their belief systems that have kept them divided around theology, such that working together to address common issues is almost impossible for some.

There is also fear or mistrust of human services providers most of whom are governmental agencies. The separation of Church and State ideology presents problems when there is no mechanism in place to address issues in an open and objective forum.

Communities are plagued by a variety of issues that can be met head on if the stakeholders could identify common issues and address the common issues and not the differences. Each partner keeps their core beliefs, but works to address the problems that create so much stress in the daily life of those "like sheep without a Shepherd."

Most communities are facing underage drinking, marijuana use, prescription drug misuse, and synthetic drug proliferation as well as educational issues in school systems. Young adults are thrown to the wolves because of the false notion that they are able to be responsible at age eighteen because they can go into the military. What happens when one is seventeen and turns eighteen that makes them able to make matured decisions?

These are common issues that all communities face not to mention violence and bullying. These commonalities can be the time when local citizens in their churches and faith based organizations can come together and take some of the stresses, harassments away from those that Christ Jesus cares so deeply for.

The Good Samaritan

One of the most convicting stories Jesus tells is of the Good Samaritan (Luke 10:25-37). Most readers will know the history of the Jewish Samaritan conflict so I will forgo that part. The application of it still needs to be studied and followed today as much as ever.

Who is your neighbor? The expert in the Law knew intellectually the first and greatest commandment as surely we do too! But, the daily application becomes another matter far too often. Jesus said, "go and do likewise." I don't believe he meant go to the assemblies and study this passage from two years old to the grave and never act on it.

I love Martin Luther King Jr.'s take on it. "The first question which the priest and the Levite asked [on the Jericho Road] was 'If I stop to help this man what will happen to me?' But...the good

Samaritan reversed the question: 'If I do not stop to help this man, what will happen to him?' "

If we don't go beyond the wall of the building for those Christ sends us to, what will happen to us? I believe the current state of things answers that for too many congregations. What has become of us is declining membership and worse, diminishing relevance as a church community that is salt of the earth and light of the world. I am not saying the people in such congregations don't matter, surely they do. I am admonishing them to relook at the core teaching of Jesus as it relates to our mission.

I began this chapter with three different scriptures of which one was Matthew 9:35-38. A look further back in this chapter is noteworthy.

In Matthew 9:1-8, Jesus steps into a boat to go to his own town. He heals a paralyzed man who had been brought to him by others. The Pharisees called him a "blasphemer." Matthew 9:9-12, Jesus calls Matthew to ministry and went to eat with him and other "sinners." The Pharisees asked the disciples of Jesus, "Why does your teacher eat with tax collectors and sinners?"

Matthew 27-34, Jesus heals a blind man and demon possessed man who was also mute and the Pharisees called Jesus' work the work of the prince of demons. So when we get to the story of Jesus going through the town and villages healing, we find him exclaiming the harvest, the community has needs he can heal, but that are not many willing to get in the trenches with them so that he can lift them out. The religious leaders were not among the workers willing to be sent among the people.

I believe most of us who have been baptized into Christ started out quite willing to do what the God of heaven sent us to do. Over the course of the years perhaps the leadership focused more on internal matters, building another building, playground renewal, foreign missions, upgrading technology, purchasing a van etc., and simply did not return to the Christ given Mission. Perhaps leadership continued to focus on the mission, but family, marriage, socioeconomic, health, conflicts and other issues overrode the messages. Whatever has happened to us as individuals and as congregations there is a rapidly changing world that is in desperate need of people who remember what it was like to be without a Savior?

The media in its various forms bring us the current news that is certainly biased; however there are alarming issues on the forefront of our communities that has the population seeking answers as never before. How are congregations prepared to tell them about gay marriage and the other communal marriages being proposed and acted into the Law of the land in way that is truthful, well researched and filled with grace and mercy as a demonstration of the community of Jesus Christ?

What are we teaching our communities about the legalization of marijuana and the possible consequences to your community? What have we learned from those who work in substance abuse prevention, treatment, law enforcement about guarding your community from bath salts and other synthetic drugs that are proliferating across class and racial lines?

What are we doing to address the large percentage of young males going into the prison Industrial Complex? Telling them to "pull up their pants and cut their hair"? Then what, get a job in a jobless market?

The Pharisees loved to look down on others, perhaps we too have turned away from the realities of today's societal issues. Yes they must obey the gospel, but is baptism the only promise of the gospel? What about Love, mercy, grace and justice?

Getting Started

"He has showed you, O Man what is good. And what does the Lord require of you? To act justly and love mercy and to walk humbly with your God." (Micah 6:8 NIV)

Define justly, love, mercy, walk and humbly. Does it begin with an assessment of where your congregation stands in its walk with God? Have you forgotten your deliverance and mission? Are you giving for the benefit of the membership? Have you built newer facilities for the members, but put not one dollar into hiring a qualified experienced person to lead the congregation into the surrounding communities? Are we planning Family Life Centers because that is the trend, but have no plans for bringing life to families?

Are you leading families to follow a disciplined prayer and devotion oriented life? Are lower income families being helped for the long term to gain employment based to skills developed through church assistance?

Is there any desire to learn about mental illness, addiction, returning veterans? Are we preparing people to learn what it means to be a homeowner in the current market?

I trust you are in some way doing all of the above through teaching even if it's not a separate "ministry."

There is contained in Deuteronomy a must read for any Christian remotely interested in the community regardless of political background which has a strong influence on a congregations outlook on community. Deuteronomy 15:4 "However there should be no poor among you, for in the land the Lord your God giving you to possess as your inheritance, he will richly bless you." Deuteronomy 15:7 If there is a poor man among your brothers in any of the towns of the land that the Lord your God is giving you, do not be hard hearted or tightfisted toward your poor brother."

Jesus said in Mark 14:7, "The poor you will always have with you, and you can help them any time you want." Our attitude is the place from which we start to become salt, light and new. The place where act justly, mercy, humbleness find life. When the attitude becomes Christ honoring, the church and community have hope of life everlasting.

Schools, human service providers, churches on the same page for the sake of the community while each carries on its mission can only become a reality when those in the church allow the love of God to override our narrow visions, fears and prejudices and transform the community filled with despair through the church. The Mission of Jesus Christ as Savior of the world delights heaven and earth because the gates of hell cannot stop the church from its appointed mission!

Kenneth Gilmore Sr.

Kenneth Gilmore Sr. has inspired audiences in twenty states and fifty cities with more than two thousand presentations. He has appeared on national radio and television throughout the United States. Kenneth Gilmore Sr. received his BS and MA from Abilene Christian University, Abilene, Texas. He has completed postgraduate work in educational leadership at Pepperdine University, Culver City, California. Kenneth is completing a doctorate in theology in Cultural Engagement and Christian Worldview at Southwestern Baptist Theological Seminary in Forth Worth, Texas. His doctoral dissertation: "*Philosophical Preaching in African-American Churches of Christ.*"

Kenneth has taught as a professor at Santa Fe Community College, and St. Leo University in Gainesville, Florida, Austin Pea State University in Clarksville, Tennessee. Kenneth is currently Lecturer in Biblical Studies at Faulkner University in Mobile, Alabama. He is a sought out motivational speaker conducting teaching conferences on relationships, finances, personal development and leadership.

Kenneth is a former staff writer for *Blueprints for Building a Better Lifestyle* a personal development curriculum published by 21st Century Christian. Kenneth is also the best selling author of several books, *The Decision is in your hand, The Leadership principle, How to Have success, The Battle for the Mind, Bring Me the Book, and Set For the Defense.*

Kenneth is married to the former Sheila Wilson and they are the proud parents of three adults Mersedes, Kenneth Jr., and Porchia, they reside in Oxford, Mississippi.

CHAPTER 3

Is the Bible God's Final Word?

Kenneth Gilmore Sr.

—⚬—

In recent times, we have seen a gradual movement away from the authority of the Bible in the contemporary church as well as in American public life. This can be seen in recent decisions by state legislatures and their redefinition of the traditional view of marriage. In philosophical ethics, the commitment to a biblical worldview is known as the divine command theory. The divine command theory is the view that whatever God commands in regards to morality or moral properties humanity is obligated to obey divine fiats. These divine commands can be expressed in God's revelation of his will in Scripture or in Paul's concept of "natural law" as revealed in Romans 1:18-23; 2:16-18. In the church today, we would expect those who have posited the existence of God, the belief in the historic creeds of the church would have no problem affirming the truth, accuracy, and authority of Scripture. But the church has also fallen victim to the idea that the Bible is not the *final authority* when it comes to addressing spiritual, moral and theological issues that confront the church.

Is the Bible God's final word and does it teach the doctrine of *Sola Scriptura? Sola Scriptura"* is the Latin term for "scripture alone." It was the principle that developed out of the Protestant Reformation movement under the leadership of Martin Luther, John Calvin who believed that the Bible was the word of God and nothing else had the right to bind or to legislate the conscience of men. In this essay I will argue that the Bible is a closed system of truth. Secondly, I will argue that the authority of Scripture was an issue that was established not only by Jesus but also by the church who had settled this matter once and for all. And third, why Scripture must remain the norm for biblical theology and ecclesiology.

I

I believe that the Bible is a closed system of truth with no new revelation being given. The chief reason for the Bible alone is the conviction that the Bible is inspired by God. It is infallible and it is inerrant. Though the church may have creeds and pronouncements, they are the works of men. These are secondary to the word of God. Paul stated clearly in 2 Timothy 3:16-17: "All scripture is given by the inspiration of God. It is profitable for doctrine, for reproof, for correction and training in righteousness, that the man of God may be perfect, thoroughly furnished unto every good work." The supreme authority rests with the Bible, not with the church, only with God. When we accept the Bible as the absolute standard of truth in matters of faith and doctrine, the Bible, and the Bible alone is God's final deposit of divine truth.

II

The word authority comes from the Greek word *Exousia* which is translated the "authority" or "power." It is employed in many different references in the New Testament. In religion today, divine authority rests on the teachings of the Apostles themselves. In the Apostolic age, the Apostles were the final authority. The Apostles had three primary and foundational functions.

First, the Apostles preached and administered God's word. Their duties were to preach, teach, and administer the affairs of the church. The preaching of the apostles rested on their association with Christ and the instruction they received from Him and included their witness to His resurrection (Acts 1:22). The church was under their immediate and direct instruction (Acts 2:42,), which consisted largely of their recollection of the teachings of Jesus, augmented by revelation of the Spirit (Ephesians 3:5). Second, in the area of administration, their functions varied. Broadly speaking, they were responsible for the life and welfare of the Christian community of the Christian church. Undoubtedly, they took their lead after the death of Christ. Third, the Apostles' responsibility was church discipline.

III

If the Apostles were the primary and authoritative witnesses to the life and teachings of Jesus, now that they have passed off the scene we are no longer living in the apostolic age, how is apostolic authority exercised in the church today? This is a critical issue, particularly in modern discussions of spiritual and religious authority, which rests on the common assumption that absolute authority belongs to Christ alone and secondary authority to the apostles. The Charismatic Movement teaches that the gifts of the apostles and prophets are still in existence today, and therefore, they have apostolic authority. Thus, some argue that the Apostles have transmitted their authority to Episcopal successors, or apostolic succession, or the gifts that we mentioned makes the church authoritative. The question is: What about the authoritative apostolic tradition that is recorded within the testimony of the New Testament?

The New Testament teaches that there is to no reason for assuming the apostolic authority has now been inherited by others. The Apostles alone are our primary witnesses to Christ, and His authority is ascribed only to them. Since the apostles are no longer here, their authority is preserved in their writing, as the inspired and normative testimony through which Christ Himself still speaks and works by the Spirit. It is through the New Testament that Jesus Christ now exercises His divine authority, imparting authoritative truth, issuing authoritative commands, and imposing an authoritative norm about which all the arguments or statements made by the church must be shaped and corrected. When we go beyond that which is written, then we get into this whole area of subjectivism, and my opinion is just as good as your opinion and my thoughts are just as good as your thoughts. When we follow the Bible, when we understand the truths of the word of God, we will not allow ourselves to be open to any speculative teaching that is outside of the canon.

IV

The divine authority of the Bible constitutes the final court of appeal in all matters of the Christian faith and practice. The divine authority of the Old Testament rests upon the testimony of Christ (Luke 24:27, 24:44). Jesus stated plainly that He would leave an unfinished revelation of truth (John 16:12). He promised that the revelation would be completed after His departure (John 16:12). He chose His apostles to receive such additional revelation as His witnesses, preachers, and teachers after His departure. Knowing beforehand what they would write, He gave to their words precisely the same authority as His own. It will help us in our understanding of the use of terms before they are employed if we can come to an understanding as to what they mean.

Revelation

There are two types of revelation in the history of Christian thought. The first refers to general revelation which develops out of Natural Theology. Natural Theology taught that in the sphere of nature God has manifested himself in the created order of the universe and the solar system as Paul clearly teaches (Romans 1:18-32). God will hold all men responsible for their violation of

Natural Law. God has implanted his moral law into the conscience of every human civilization. The second type is Special revelation where God has specifically revealed his will and purpose in the writings of sacred Scripture (2 Timothy 3:16-17) It is in Special revelation where God reveals to man his need of salvation and the provision God has made through his son Jesus Christ.

The word "revelation" may be defined as the act of God by which He communicates to the mind of man truth not known before. This truth is incapable of being discovered by the mind of man unaided by the Holy Spirit (1 Corinthians 2:14ff, Ephesians 3:1ff).

Inspiration

By inspiration of the Scriptures, we mean that special divine influence upon the minds of the biblical writers, and render them *infallible* in the communication of divine truth. Their production, apart from errors of transcription and when rightly interpreted, constituted the infallible rule of faith and practice. For believers the New Testament is "inspired literature," is different from any other great literary works. Inspiration is a theological term that concerns the nature of the Spirit of God upon the biblical writers to produce a divinely authoritative writings. It is derived from the Vulgate (Latin) usage of the word *inspiro* (e.g., Gen. 2:7; 2 Timothy 3:16; 2 Peter 1:21) and the noun *inspiratio* (e.g. Job 32:8; Psalm 18:15; Acts 17:25). In Matthew 22:43; Jesus speaks of David writing Psalm 110 was "inspired by the Spirit. (*en pneumatic, Greek*) In Mark 12:36; (parallel passage) was "inspired by the Holy Spirit: (*en to pneumatic to hagio*). In 2 Timothy 3:16; says "all scripture is inspired by God" (*pasa graphe theopneutos, divinitus inspirata*) inspiration (breathed into by God) the product of the creative breath of God. Scripture is a divine product according to the biblical writers. The "Breath of God" is a symbolic way of referring to his almighty power and "by the word of the Lord" is almost the same as found in Psalm 33:6 "...were the heavens made, and all their host by the

49

breath of his mouth." (See 2 Peter 1:21 for inclusion by Peter of Paul's writing as "inspired").

Illumination

The word "illumination," is the divine quickening of the human mind, which enables one to understand the very words of Scripture as being inspired. The testimony of the Old Testament writers bears witness to God's verbal inspiration, as well as writers in the New Testament. Peter and Paul attested to the fact that God had given them a word to communicate to their particular audience that they might fully understand what God's will is. So when we speak about revelation and inspiration, we are speaking about God's ultimate authority, which rests in the word of God—the Bible. If we are going to live according to God's will, then the Bible has to be the ultimate authority and Supreme Court in all matters of religion. Every question must be settled by the word of God.

Sources of Authority

The Old Testament

Prior to the establishment of the church, Judaism possessed what was essentially a "canon." Jesus himself paved the way for the Church's acceptance of the "Jewish" canon by His constant appeal to the Old Testament. His basic affirmation was that the Old Testament Scripture, as a whole, and in its parts had come to fulfillment in Him. (See Matthew 5:17; John 5:39; Romans 3:31). By continuing this "Christological" interpretation of the Old Testament, the Church proclaimed that it not Judaism was the proper interpreter of the Old Testament. For Paul the Old Testament could only be read meaningfully with respect to the historical appearance of Jesus Christ. (2 Corinthians 3:6ff; cf. 1 Corinthians 10:1ff.)

The Spirit

The "Spirit" gave to holy men of old the inspiration that led to the production of the components of the Old Testament canon. (See 2 Peter 1:21 and 2 Timothy 3:16) So, the expectation of the "age of the Spirit" was that particularly with the historical presence of Christ and the descent of the Spirit, that new and more inspired writings would be realized.

The Lord

The Ultimate authority for the early church was the living authority of the risen Lord Himself. On a number of occasions Paul refers directly to a "word of the Lord" (1 Thessalonians 4:15; 1 Corinthians 7:10; 9:14; 11:23; cf. Acts 20:35). Similar direct appeal to the teaching of Jesus continued into the postapostolic age (cf., e.g., 1 Clem 13:2; 46:8; Didache 8:2; 9:5; Ignatius of Smyrna 3:2 Phil 2:3; 7:2; Barn 5:9).

The Apostles

The apostles constituted a fourth source of authority for the Church from its earliest day. The authority of the apostles were already granted to them before the resurrection (cf. Mark 3:14 6:7). After the resurrection the Apostles manifested this authority in their dual witness to the resurrection of Jesus Christ and to His words (cf. Acts 1:21ff; 1 Corinthians 9:1ff.). For this task they received the gift of the Spirit. Paul as example of his authority tells Thessalonians to read his letter to all brethren (1 Thessalonians 5:27), or directs the church that his letters be circulated beyond its original destination (Colossians 4:16).

The depth of his authority can be seen in his blunt demand that fellowship be withdrawn from those who refuse to obey his commands (2 Thessalonians 3:14; cf. v. 6). His own command is secondary to the "word of the Lord" (cf., 1 Corinthians 7:12ff; 9:17ff.) yet it is nonetheless a command that may stand alongside the command of Jesus. Rejecting the apostles is tantamount to rejecting Christ Himself. (Cf. Mark 8:38).

Criteria Used to Determine Scripture

1. *The test of Apostolicity:*

Was the book the work of an Apostle, or if not did it have an Apostle as its authority?

2. *The test of Universality:*

Was the writing widely circulated and approved by Christians in general?

3. *The test of doctrinal Content:*

No book was admitted which taught anything contrary to the rule of faith. On the basis of this test, most of the apocryphal and pseudepigraphical books were eliminated.

4. *Test of Intrinsic Worth:*

That is the spirituality and sublimity of the books. This does not means they were simply inspiring and worthwhile to read, but they had a dynamic power to transform human life.

5. *The test of Inspiration:*

Did the book give evidence of being divinely inspired? This was the ultimate criterion of canonicity. Everything finally had to give way to it. An important observation not to be over looked is that the formation of the canon was a process shaped and guided by the Providence of God. In other words, God who inspired the writings also had a hand in the selection of His Books over those that were noninspired writings. The New Testament came to us naturally, with minimal interference by man. It marched relentlessly through history with such orderly progression that it is tough to quarrel with its claim of divine Inspiration. Thus, the Holy Spirit quickened the instincts of devout men, aided discernment between the genuine and the spurious, and thus led to gradual, harmonious and, in the end, unanimous conclusions. The Holy Spirit not only inspired the writings of the Books, He inspired the selecting of the books. A clear reading of the New Testament reveals that the authors themselves assumed a canonical authority. In other words they understood themselves to be under the Inspiration of the Holy Spirit.

It is vital to remember that being accepted into the canon did not elevate a book to Scripture. It simply recognized that the book already was Scripture. It has been well said that the Bible is not an authorized collection of books, but a collection of authorized books.

Benjamin A. Griffin

Benjamin A. Griffin earned an AB in Bible from the Bellview Preaching Training School in 1987, 1992-2000 his BA, MA in Ministry and Doctorate of Ministry in Leadership and Organizational Development from the Theological University of America. In 2013, he earned his MA of Ministry in Leadership Studies, from Lancaster Bible College and Graduate School. He completed MPA course work in Strategic Management at UNCW in Wilmington, NC. He is founder of IFC Ministry and Southeastern Institute for Church Leadership. He is nationally certified as a Bereavement Facilitator 2001, as a Chaplain in 2009 and as a Church Consultant in 2011. He has authored and published the book "Christian Living."

Ben also possesses a comprehensive background in organizational training and development; in community education, outreach and development. For more than thirty years he has worked in Ministerial Leadership and a consulting capacity by helping churches, by designing and implementing budgets; composition and implementation of leadership and outreach training plans and manuals.

He is married with three adult children, two teenagers and four grandchildren. He presently preaches in Wilmington North Carolina, at the Wilmington Central church of Christ

CHAPTER 4

The Nature and Necessity of Church Leadership
(Spiritual, Biblical, and Ecclesial)

Benjamin A. Griffin

—ᴍ—

Introduction

We are living in exciting days for the Lord's church. Throughout our great brotherhood, great progress is being made in all areas of the work assigned to the church by the Master. Across the land, congregations are moving forward by faith as more and more people are becoming involved in the ongoing growth in the local churches. Why is this happening? In a word—Leadership! This is the key. Men of outstanding abilities are involved in leadership on all levels in local congregations. This has produced a renewed interest in leadership training, as the man in the pew has become excited about the work in the church and his role in it. He is no longer content to sit still and let "George do it." Workshops, seminars, classes, training sessions, and a host of other efforts are being used to prepare members of the Lord's church to be more productive leaders. As one Elder expressed, "We are taking leadership training more seriously now than we have ever taken it."

Since the Church is the primary vehicle by which God's agenda is accomplished, then the primary engine that drives the church are Christ-focused, Christ-honoring leaders. The one enduring issue that continues to plague the church is not a lack of resources, not a lack of strategies, not a lack of programs, but a lack of leadership. What does it take to lead a church that is growing spiritually and numerically as God intended? It certainly takes more than the desire to grow. Most leaders struggle with how to motivate and involve members in the midst of busy lifestyles. Many leaders find it difficult to concentrate on their key biblical roles and responsibilities with so many peripheral issues demanding their attention.

Leaders are essential to the work of the church, and need to be developed in competency and character, which includes the development of one's gifts. The church needs to put more effort into developing leaders who are Christ-focused, highly competent men of character who know how to reproduce their lives through the lives of others. Leaders, no matter how naturally gifted some might be, still need to be developed. There is no shortage of opinions as to how we can and must reverse these trends and make healthy, growing churches the rule rather than the exception.

After spending nearly ten years in the Army, I acquired (military) leadership, was employed in sales, marketing and management (corporate leadership), being active in church work for over thirty years (spiritual leadership), educational leadership, and as a husband and father of five children and four grandchildren (domestic leadership).

Leadership is an inevitable calling and can be acquired through many avenues. You may already be in leadership and doing a good job of leading, but **good leaders** are always striving to become even

better leaders. Leadership appears to be glamorous, but is more often lonely and thankless.

I will attempt to address the subject from a general and specific point of view. General: what is leadership as it pertains to everyone regardless of their status in life? Specific: what is leadership as it pertains to those who take up church work, ministry, and spiritual leadership?

My hope in this chapter is to strike a cord in the hearts of brethren, both young and old, the active and the up and coming, who are stimulated with the thought of leading others. As we shall see, the best **Leaders** are actually **Servants**. "God wants leaders who will match the mountains of life."

Nature of Leadership

There have been thousands of books and articles written; workshop, seminars and retreats conducted to gain a better understanding of this all encompassing subject. Men are reluctant to accept both brief and lengthy definitions and descriptions given concerning leadership because of their own ideas. I am among those who constantly search for what we think is the paramount meaning and the ultimate way of it, only to find myself doing more searching.

And as earlier stated, my leadership experience has been attained from a variety of avenues: military, domestic, educational, business and ecclesial. However, there are many serious students of this subject who have attempted to define it.

Secular Perspective:

"A leader is a person with certain qualities of personality and character, which are appropriate to the general situation, and supported by a degree of relevant technical knowledge and experience. A leader is one who is able to provide the necessary functions to guide a group towards the further realization of its purpose, while maintaining and building its unity as a team; doing all this in the right ration or proportion with the contributions of others members of the team." John Adair, Action-Centered Leadership

Spiritual Perspective:

"Leadership is a dynamic process in which a man or women with God-given capacity influences a specific group of God's people toward His purpose for that group."
J. Robert Clinton, The Making of a Leader

"A Christian leader is someone who is called by God to lead and possess virtuous characteristics and effectively motivates, mobilizes resources and directs people toward the fulfillment of a jointly embraced vision from God."
George Barna, The Second Coming of the Church

"Private leadership must come before Public leadership"

Every man must first govern self and govern his own family, a small society he must master before he governs a larger one, the church (1 Timothy 3:4, 5; 4:10-16). Someone said that the home is the boot camp for church leadership. Everyone must use training wheels at some point in life, at least for a little while. The man has a role all of his own that none other can perform but him. He is obligated to be both the physical and spiritual head of the family. God has placed this responsibility upon him. The home is the first institution and God placed the man to be the head of it (Joshua 14:15; Acts 10:1-2; 16:30-34).

The word "husband" is but a contraction of two words "house" and "band." Truly, the "husband" is the "house-band" a band of strength around the house: upholding, protecting, nourishing and keeping it together. Therefore, the man must ensure stability, peace and order in the home. God gave him this divine role.

"Let Him be a Leader of Integrity!"

"Bad men will, when good men won't" Judges 9:8-16. This is one of the few parables in the Old Testament. It shows an engagement of selecting a king from among upright men to reign over the people of God in Shechem. Unfortunately, because, none of the upright men would sacrifice their comfort zone to lead God's people, by default it allowed an unjust, unrighteous, and unfair man ascend to the kingship. Whenever those who know to do the right thing refuse to, opens the door for evil. Churches must ensure that they are raising men of integrity, so when the time comes to replace or install new leaders, it will have those who know to take the lead, and not leave the Lord's work in the hands of men of ill will. Leaders with integrity are a rare breed within a group of citizens, whose utmost concern is, "What is in it for me?" A selfish society does not always select a leader for their integrity, but for their ability to manipulate a quick fix for chronic problems. It is shortsightedness that can set back a generation, because of their leader's greed and corruption.

However, men of integrity understand the big picture of principled leadership and they value fear of God, trustworthiness and honest economics. A leader of integrity looks out over the long term and discovers what is best for the culture, its citizens, churches and families. There is a resolve to do the right thing, with the right people, for the right reasons. Leaders of integrity integrate uprightness with their quiet influence.

A leader can't be committed one day and uninterested the next.

Spiritual Leadership

Spiritual Leadership as well as leadership in general, is often hard to define. We think we know what it is but it's often hard to put into words. I think that sometimes we know more of what it is not, rather than what it is. We tend to think of people as leaders who have position, skill, knowledge, prestige, social status, or a great personality. But they are not great leaders if they cannot motivate people and if they do not have the attitude and action necessary to move themselves and others to accomplish the goal at hand. This is especially true for Spiritual Leadership because men of faith have always been people of action. Spiritual Leadership action requires faith because setting and securing goals is certainly an act of faith.

While spiritual leadership involves many of the same principles as general leadership, spiritual leadership has certain distinctive qualities that must be understood and practiced if spiritual leaders are to be successful. The spiritual leader's task is to move people from where they are to where God wants them to be. This is influence. Once spiritual leaders understand God's will, they make every effort to move their followers from following their own agendas to pursuing God's purposes. People who fail to move people to God's agenda have not led. Spiritual leaders depend on the Holy Spirit. But Jesus was willing to do even that (John 13:12-17). True spiritual leadership, with a spirit of humility and service, will cause people to follow you because they want to, not because they have to. Genuine humility and spiritual leadership is attractive.

Spiritual leaders can influence all people, not just God's people. God's agenda applies to the marketplace as well as the meeting place. God can use them to exert significant godly influence upon unbelievers. Spiritual leaders work from God's agenda. The greatest obstacle to effective spiritual leadership is people pursing their own agendas, rather then God's will.

Spiritual leadership is the opposite of what most people think. Spiritual leadership is servant leadership. Jesus Christ Himself taught, "Just as the Son of Man did not come to be served, but to served and give his life for as a ransom for many" (Matthew 20:28).

Spiritual leadership involves humbling yourself and doing the tasks that no one else wants to do. In Jesus' days, the act of washing feet was to be assigned to the lowest of servants. Spiritual leadership positively influences spiritual well-being as group members model the values of altruistic love to one another as they jointly develop a common vision. This provides the foundation for generating hope/faith and a willingness to do what it takes in pursuit of a vision, which produces a sense of calling which will make a difference.

Concurrently, as leaders and followers engage in this process and gain a sense of mutual care and concern through the experience of altruistic love, workers gain a sense of membership, belonging and community as they feel understood and appreciated. So then, in our understanding, spiritual leadership is about tending relationships in four spheres: within ourselves (internal), between individuals (interpersonal), within structures (institutional), and among cultures (ideological).

It is about creating and maintaining alignment among these spheres—so that what is best at every level can be drawn out for the good of everyone, however, with Gods' agenda as the standard.

The Necessity of Church Leadership

There are few things more important to human activity than leadership. Effective leadership helps our nation through times of perils. It makes a business organization successful. It enables a not-for-profit organization to fulfill its mission. The effective leadership of parents enables children to grow strong and healthy and become productive adults. Leadership sustains our faith in God. The absence of leadership is equally dramatic in its effects. Without leadership, organizations move slowly, stagnate, and lose their way.

Problems of implementation are really issues about how leaders influence behavior, change the course of events, and overcome resistance. Leadership is crucial in implementing decisions successfully. Each of us recognizes the importance of leadership when we vote for our political leaders. We realize that it matters who is in office, so we participate in a contest, an election, to choose the best candidate.

Leadership can be used for good or ill. Sometimes people in business have great leadership skills, but put them to terrible uses. The danger of that leadership like that will be perverted is why ethics are so important to good leadership. Ethics are the inner compass that directs a person toward what is right and fair. Only if a person has an inner ethical compass can he or she be sure that leadership qualities will not turn to evil ends.

Ecclesial Leadership

Ecclesial Leadership is the process whereby an individual answers God's call, follows Christ's example and influence others to fulfill the will of God personally and corporately (Bayes, 2010).

Titus was a Gentile (Gal. 2:3); but unto Paul, he was a partner and fellow-worker, and son after the common faith (2 Cor. 8:23; Titus 1:4). Having spent time with Paul in Ephesus, Titus served the Lord in various places; and then even in making that journey to see the effects of Paul's' first letter to that troubled congregation. In the letter that bears his name, he was serving the Lord in Crete, an island in the Mediterranean Sea. It is 158 miles long and varies in width in places from 5 to 50 miles. Paul addresses three particular topics in this letter: church organization, holy living, and discipline. It is the matter of church organization that we will discuss.

Titus 1:5-9 "For this cause left I thee in Crete, that thou shouldest set in order the things that are wanting, and ordain elders in every city, as I had appointed thee: 1:6 If any be blameless, the husband of one wife, having faithful children not accused of riot or unruly. 1:7 For a bishop must be blameless, as the steward of God; not self-willed, not soon angry, not given to wine, no striker, not given to filthy lucre; 1:8 But a lover of hospitality, a lover of good men, sober, just, holy, temperate; 1:9 Holding fast the faithful word as he hath been taught,

that he may be able by sound doctrine to exhort and to convince the gainsayers.

We notice that the admonition of Paul was to address the things that were wanting. From the book, we can determine that this embraced several things. At the head of the list was of course the need for competent godly leadership. There was also a realization that false teachers were going unchallenged. Various members of the church were not assuming their responsibilities: He addresses the older men, older women, younger women and younger men. There was also the general challenge to the church to live a godly life. He even addresses the need for the members of the church to be law abiding citizens. And also follows up with concerns about those who were causing trouble.

Therefore, Titus is told to ordain or appoint elders. Vines states of the word: that appoint means "to appoint a person to a position." What is important in regard to such an appointment is that the individuals to be appointed must meet certain requirements given of God. Scripture is inspired of God, therefore what is penned here is from the Holy Spirit, and is not to be taken lightly.

It is important to understand that men are not qualified because they are appointed, but appointed because they are qualified. We also note that the inspired admonition was that elders were to be appointed in every city, bolstered by Paul's making it clear that this was an apostolic command. The phrases: every church, every city, makes it abundantly evident that elders are to preside in every congregation of the Lord's church.

The nature of ecclesial leadership is to tap into the fundamental needs of both leaders and followers for spiritual well-being through calling and membership, to create vision and value across all levels and departments of the organization.

Vision refers to a picture of the future with such implicit or explicit commentary on why people should strive to create that future.

Moreover, a compelling vision energizes workers, gives meaning to work, garners commitment, and establishes a standard of excellence. In mobilizing people, a vision must have broad appeal, define the organizations destination and journey, reflecting ideals, and encourage hope and faith.

For ecclesial leadership, Altruistic Love is defined as a sense of wholeness, harmony, and well-being produced through care, concern and appreciation for both self and others. As a key component of unit and organizational culture, altruistic love defines the set of key values, assumptions, understandings and ways of thinking considered to be morally right that are shared by group members and taught to new members. Spiritual leaders embody and abide in these values through their everyday attitudes and behavior.

Hope/Faith is desire with the expectation of fulfillment. Faith adds certainty to hope. It is a firm belief in something for which there is no visible evidence. It is based on values, attitudes, and behaviors that demonstrate absolute certainty and trust that what is desired and expected will come to pass. People with hope/faith have a vision of where they are going, and how to get there; they are willing to face opposition and endure hardship and suffering, in order to achieve their goals. Hope/faith is thus the source for the conviction the organizations vision will be fulfilled and is demonstrated through action or work.

Calling refers to the experience of transcendence or how one makes a difference through service to others and, in doing so, finds meaning and purpose in life. Many people seek not only competence and mastery to realize their full potential through their work, but also a sense that work has some social meaning or value.

The term "calling" has long been used as one of the defining characteristics of a professional. It is also used in scripture to define ones vocation as a Christian. The challenge for the organizational leaders, which is addressed through the spiritual leadership model, is how to develop this same sense of calling in its worker through task and involvement and goal identification.

Membership encompasses a sense of belonging and community in which and through we seek to be understood and appreciated. Having a sense of understanding and appreciation is largely a matter of interrelationships and connections through interaction, and thus membership. Ultimately, we grow greater, live longer, and more meaningful in proportion as we identify ourselves with the larger social life that surrounds us.

Biblical Leadership Begins with a Biblical Eldership

Tracing the history of New Testament church leadership, God initially gave the church apostles and prophets. These leaders did the foundational work after the birth of the Church (Ephesians 2:20; 4:11). As the church grew, the apostles handed the baton of leadership to elders. Elders were appointed for each church (Acts 11:23; 15:6, 23; 20:17, 28). These men were given responsibility to shepherd and oversee local churches (1 Peter 5:1-4).

There is no indication in the New Testament that the office of apostle was meant to continue beyond the first century. In fact, in the restricted sense, no one today would meet the qualifications for apostle (Acts 1:21-22; 1 Cor. 15:8). And since the early church gave itself to the teaching for the apostles (Acts 2:42; now found in the NT epistles), we would have to ask what level of authority we would give to the teaching of people who want to be viewed as apostles. Appointing apostles for the Churches is not an action supported by the pattern of the New Testament.

Does a clear pattern for church government emerge from the pages of the New Testament? Of course it is. The New Testament reveals a pattern in which each local Church was placed under the spiritual care of a plurality of godly leaders called elders. When churches disregard this pattern, they fail to meet God's standard and they fall short.

Conclusion:

Jesus Christ is the ultimate example of spiritual leadership. When most people think of leadership, they picture a military officer giving out orders or an employer closely supervising his employees, making sure all the work gets done. These aspects can be a part of leadership, but they are not the essence of spiritual leadership.

Current leadership theories focus to varying degrees on one or more aspects of the physical, mental or emotional elements of human interaction in organization, and neglect the spiritual component. Thus, spiritual leadership generates hope/faith in the organization's vision that keeps followers looking forward to the future. Ecclesial leadership requires that an organization's culture be based on values of altruistic love. This must be demonstrated through leader's attitudes and behavior and produces a sense of membership—that part of spiritual well-being that gives on a sense of being understood and appreciated. Ultimately, the nature and necessity of church leadership will be of greater effectiveness when it is understood and implemented from the Bible's perspective.

Stanley Hubbard

Stanley Hubbard is the Senior Minister of the Word for the Kingsley Terrace Church of Christ in Indianapolis, IN. Under his ministry, Kingsley Terrace has more than doubled in size. Stanley is a graduate of Preston Road School of Preaching in Dallas, TX. He received his BA in Bible from Heritage University and received his Masters in Ministry from Southern Christian University. He received his second Masters degree in Marriage and Family Therapy and has a Master of Divinity in Marriage and family Therapy. He has ministered with congregations in Texas, Alabama and North Carolina before moving to Indiana. Brother Hubbard and his wife, Laura, have three children and six grandchildren.

Stanley also travels worldwide on numerous workshops, revivals, gospel meetings and lectureships. He has traveled extensively conducting Singles Workshops, Leadership Workshops, Blended Families and Marriage and family Seminars/Workshops from Bermuda, Bahamas, Jamaica, Okinawa, Japan, Italy, Quebec, Canada, and Central America to all over the United States.

CHAPTER 5

The Preacher, the Pew, and the Process
Strategies for Finding the Right Fit

Stanley J. Hubbard

—⁓—

*T*he story is told of the church that had a pattern of changing preachers every two to three years. A young preacher went there and began to preach. After being at the congregation for about four years, he began to feel that his great success had to do with his great talent and great ability. He spoke to one of the brethren who participates in leading and asked him, "I know that for many years this church had a history of changing preachers every two to three years. I have outlasted many preachers who have been here before. To what do you contribute my success of being able to be here this long? Is it my great teaching, my great preaching or some other aspect of my ministry?" The brother responded by saying, "in all honesty, preacher you are right. We have never liked preachers much and typically like preaching even less. I contribute your success to the fact that since we do not like preachers or *preaching, you are the closest thing to a no preaching preacher we have ever had."*

As humorous as this may be, it is at times uncomfortably close to the truth in some places. If you do not know what you are aiming for, how can you expect to hit it? In the USA there is a constant rotation of preachers moving from location to location. The unfortunate reality is that many congregations have no idea of how to evaluate a preacher and many preachers have no idea on how to evaluate a church. This often accounts for the number of splits and the constant movement of preachers. Far too often, the process of a congregation gaining a preacher consists of having him send a resume and a sermon tape. If he makes the first cut they have him come in and preach. Afterward, the church, often through leadership, congregational input or communication with certain members, decides based on the level of enjoyment of the sermon and chemistry, and whether there is enough in common for a match. By contrast, for many preachers, the process for evaluating a congregation is based on congregational reputation and how much they pay. For many preachers, the major determining factor is an increase in pay. Before the process of interviewing the preacher or looking for a church begins, it is important to understand the three types of preachers and congregations. I have heard it stated that there are three types of preachers which should match the three types of churches.

UNDERTAKERS. An undertaker deals with death. Undertaker congregations, like the term, is a church that is heading to the grave. It is a church where membership and the church at large are in the process of declining or dying. Every year their membership is dwindling and they are losing more members. They often do not see the cause of their dilemma. Sometimes it is due to economic flight or cultural-flight (congregational change due to racial, residential or economic changes). Sometimes, a church is dying because they have archaic approaches or are living in the memories from their glory days. It may not be their fault. They may be in an area that has lost employment opportunities and younger members moves away for economic survival. These congregations are dying and often need preachers who are starting in their ministry, close to retirement or men who are willing to stay and love them until the last member is gone.

CARETAKERS. Caretakers typically have a job of showing care for and sustaining someone in their present condition. Caretaker congregations are looking for someone who will marry off their children and bury their parents. These congregations often have a pattern of operation that they are comfortable with and do not want change. The majority of congregations have a caretaker mentality. They may often find themselves having very little fluctuation in what they do or how they do it. You can worship there and leave, come back in ten years and upon your return, it may seem as though this church is in a time warp. No matter how much time passes, they basically have the same membership and very few things are different (i.e. outside of who has died and who is now married with children). They are often comfortable and need a preacher who is fine with the status quo. They may accept small, modifiable changes, but tend to not have much change in their leadership. It typically takes these groups a long time to make simple decisions and an even longer time to implement simple change. Many preachers become extremely frustrated because they can be slow when it comes to actually implementing business practices. They may have programs or activities that began thirty years ago that no longer work and are no longer effective, but they continue to do them because they always have. They may even reject new ideas because they have never tried any before.

RISK-TAKERS. Risk-takers in life are people who embrace novelty and diversity. Risk-taker congregations are constantly being made over and remade. It is not peculiar to show up five to ten years later and notice a significant change in appearance, membership, focus, leadership and even plans. These churches and preachers do not feel threatened by change. They aren't intimidated by church development. They look for ways to help members find the ministry and gifts that God has given them. They won't change the word but they challenge methods and techniques that are outdated. They are willing to look at what the church does and focus on what is working. They believe that there is a place and function for every member and continue to seek ways to add opportunities for service. The leaders in these congregations can have one meeting, make a decision and implement the plan that same day. They don't need a preacher who is going to try to remake them into the church of the 1960s-1980s. They need a preacher who is willing to challenge them to strive for greatness. They will be open to exploring how they can impact the world and not just the corner they are sitting on. They may irritate other congregations because of their size or multifaceted views of doing things differently which breaks the status quo. They are more independent in thoughts and actions and may not wait for brotherhood approval.

HOW A PREACHER EVALUATES A CHURCH
(THE PULPIT)

How is a preacher to evaluate a congregation? First consider that each congregation, like each person, has its own personality. Just like each person is different, so is each congregation. The psychology of a group is similar to the psychology of an individual. If a person has murdered before, they may murder again. If someone has stolen before, they may steal again. Just like a person will do what a person has already done, a church will do what a church has done. If a congregation has in its history to release a preacher without any forewarning, it may do so in its future. If a congregation has a tendency to change preachers every two to three years it will probably do that in its future. If a congregation has had in its history a preacher who has been there for thirty years, they will comfortably do that in their future. When I do workshops on dating, I explain that you should not begin dating until you know why you are dating. One may date, looking for a lifetime partner, while another's goal is to have a friend to enjoy at the movies. As you begin to look at various congregations, it is important to understand what environment best suits you. It is important that the preacher understands his "Philosophy of Ministry." In a website article (befctv.org) on an overview of a "Philosophy of Ministry" by Neal Laybourne, he defines a Philosophy of Ministry.

Neal defines the term. "A Philosophy of Ministry is *a statement of _how_ you will accomplish your purpose and _why_ you do what you do in ministry.* Therefore, your "Philosophy of Ministry" is a response to a series of questions that challenge you to think about your own strengths and weaknesses. It explains why you do what you do. One needs to consider what their main objective is in preaching and teaching. Of all the things that drive those in ministry, what do you do best? Just like each person is different, so is each preacher. I know that the perception is that every preacher should find his strength in evangelism and congregational growth. The reason every congregation does not grow is because evangelism is not the strength of all preachers. The reason members attend different congregations is because people tend to follow the path and direction of their leader and congregation which most closely fits their comfort and spiritual ideology. You cannot expect any more out of the followers than you can from their leader. As the leader does, so will his people. After five years, most congregations can begin to mirror the personality of its preacher. The congregation's ideology, personality and attitude ends up being shaped by these qualities in the preacher unless the relationship between the two is strained. If you have growth, the type of growth you have will be based on the type of preacher you have. In a graduate course with Dr. Earl Edwards at Freed Hardeman University, he shared with us several types of congregational growths. These types of growth do not necessarily bring in more money or more people. They do, however, give insight to the distinction of different groups and the strength of different preachers. The types of growth are the following:

Internal growth—Every child of God and every congregation should be growing spiritually. This is growth in grace, knowledge and spiritual maturity. Every church should anticipate this type of growth but it is not a guarantee. If one only feeds on milk they will always be a baby.

External Growth—There can be an increase in external energy around a congregation. This encompasses numerical growth in attendance, offering, membership, or enrollment. This can include expanding your land base, building a new facility, buying more property, vans, busses, renovating and other expansions.

Biological Growth—Congregations which have young families will often notice an increase due to procreation. This is numerical growth due to members producing offspring. Children do not remain children. Respect the value that these young families bring. These young ones grow up and expand your base by having their own children. Many large congregations began with large families.

Transfer Growth—We live in a transient society. Many people are moving to your city or just want to move to a different congregation. This not about someone being a "sheep hustler," it's about displaced sheep who have gotten lost or feel they would be best served or offer better service at a different location. A reality of ministry in these present times is that people will attend where they want to and will not ask for anyone's permission. People tend to move to a place because they feel frustrated where they are or they feel a special affinity to the preacher. However, people are fickle, so be aware that all transfers are not created equal. Some can be a blessing and some will feel like a curse.

Conversion Growth—This is numerical growth by winning lost souls and assimilating them into the body. We often suggest that this is the only legitimate growth. It is a fundamental sign of biblical growth and it indicates a healthy congregation. There are congregations which never grow in size but have constant conversions. Their strength is to reach the lost, but developing the babes and assimilating them is not their strength. One church may plant and another may water, but all increase is in the hands of the Lord.

Expansion Growth—This is growth of planting new congregations nationally or internationally, starting new congregational sites and/or new classes. These congregations are committed to the call of Jesus to go into all the world. When I preached in North Carolina we developed and started three new congregations. This growth blesses the morale of a congregation and adds to the kingdom, but does not initially bring any direct benefit to the host church. It takes a special level of spiritual maturity to work on this level.

Community Growth—This will cause the group to be better known or making a larger impact in the city where they are located. This growth increases your churches visibility in your city or community due to involvement and impact. It may be due to the church becoming more political or its social impact on the community's needs. This growth will make a church a household name.

It is important that you understand which type of growth you can trigger. Most preachers can build a congregation by developing many of these types of growth. Part of your "Philosophy of Ministry" will help you to understand the best type of congregations to match your strength. When a preacher is considering going to work with a congregation, there are many factors that need to be evaluated:

COMMUNITY

As a preacher considers a congregation, he needs to also assess the city the church is in as well. It is not just you moving here; your children and wife are coming with you. So you must consider the schools in this city compared to education and colleges that your children will need to compete with in their future and what will you do to offset any concerns. Is the city overly populated with adult/sex businesses? These generally increase sex, violent and property crimes. Is the church building near these structures? This could suggest heavy deviant behavior. Is this city overrun with gang activity and will that impact your children at their present age or in the near future? Does your family feel safe and valued in this environment? It is important to have the conversation with them since your leadership is being examined by how your whole family is impacted. Will your children initially be the only Christian children in this congregation and how are you going to keep them growing until that changes? What are the relationships with local congregations in this city and how will that bless or hinder your ministry? Are there any special concerns about other religious groups that may impact your success? Who has a stronghold in this city and how are you going to impact that? If its Muslims, Jehovah Witness, Seventh-Day Adventist or whoever they may be, you need to consider how your strengths will add to your success or what will you need to do to be successful here.

LEADERSHIP

Seek to understand the men who presently lead. You are making a commitment to work with them. You will have difficulty being successful in your work if your philosophy is they must lose in order for you to win. Do they expect you to work for them or with them? Do they respect the Bible as the authority and plan of God? Will they fight for tradition or scripture? Can you love them into change even if it takes years? You must consider if you can be patient with the personalities, quirks and differences of those who are leading now. If you do not feel you can respect them or work with them, do not even consider taking the work.

It is important that the preacher knows and understands himself. Is your strength in building families, developing men, evangelism, debating, counseling, community issues, unifying the brethren, connecting with the sick, administrating, youth, programs or projects? Whatever your strength is, you must view congregations based on what you can achieve and their openness to accept your vision to improve and impact this area of their existence. A preacher with a good understanding of his strengths may change a congregational emphasis and build the type of growth that fits his ministry style. Every church and every preacher is not created equal. They have different personalities and a different emphasis from each other. Again, this is why different members are attracted to different ministries in the same city.

This is intended to give you insight to help explain our differences and how to not make false assumptions about a congregation. Sometimes a woman will say "I just want to get married"; however, any woman who wants to get married can get married any time she wants. There are hundreds of men being released from prison who would love to move in and make himself at home. However, what she really wants is a healthy relationship that leads to marriage. In like manner, you are not just looking for a place to preach, you looking for a place that will work with your special God-given gifts. Before you begin the process, you must know your strengths. You can only create out of you what exists inside you. If you love others, you will tend to create a loving environment. If you are often in tension and turmoil, you will create an environment that matches that tension. If you are friendly and loving, you will attract people who are friendly and loving. If you are basically distant, you will create an environment of distance. Whatever the leader has within, the followers will show without.

FACILITY

Haggai 2:2 This is what the Lord Almighty says: "These people say, 'The time has not yet come for the Lord's house to be built.'" 3 Then the word of the Lord came through the prophet Haggai: 4 "Is it a time for you yourselves to be living in your paneled houses, while this house remains a ruin?"

This addresses the heart of a people. I often have a concern that people who do not take care of Gods things will not take care of

God's people. Often, you can tell much about a people based on where they worship. Just like you can tell which is most important to someone by looking at how they manage their car, yard, vacation, family, time, talent and treasures. If the place is dirty, unkept, with a rusty old, raggedy van and junk around the building, it is the first visible sign of either their lack of concern for the things of God or their lack of awareness. It is important to identify if it is negligence, unawareness or a lack of concern. When members drive up with brand new Hummers, Jags and BMWs but the church has a rusty, raggedy van, it may show the lack of concern they have for those who do not have transportation or a lack of awareness of the impression they are leaving in their expressions of their love for God. Often, older, controlling men are not as concerned about the aesthetics of a congregation. Women who have influence at home will want to continue to change the home environment. Women have a tendency to want to change out furnishings, refresh flowers and beautify a facility. So a facility that has been beautified may tell you something about the involvement of the women and the emphasis the men place on control.

MEMBERSHIP AGE

The age of the membership is important to notice. It tells you if the congregation is becoming an Undertaker Church. The age of the men in the congregation can tell you much about how inclusive they are. If there is a large gap between the ages of twenty to forty-five or an absence of young men under the age of thirty, it could be a sign of an environment where older men are too focused on control to the extent that younger men feel devalued. It takes work to make young men feel a part of a congregation. Paul understood this and that is why he has so many men he mentored in the 1st century church. It takes special effort and attention to have a Timothy, John Mark, Titus, Epaphroditus, Trophimus and the list goes on. Remember however, that like tends to attract like. The preacher will often attract people that fit his ideology and in his age range. Men tend to not get involved in things that they do not do well. Many men avoid getting involved with the congregation because it is often seen as a place for women to gather, read and talk. Men tend to focus on action more than traditional classes. Getting young men involved will require an intentional plan that teaches them how men bond and work for the Lord together. It's important to know if this congregation will feel threatened by the involvement and challenges that come with young men who may not want to function like they are sixty-year-olds.

INTERVIEW

A good way to think about the church/preacher interview is to imagine it as a date. When a preacher is invited to come to talk to a congregation about becoming their preacher, this is a date. As in any date, you will be treated better on the date than you traditionally will in the marriage. After all, the purpose of the date is to impress you. It is important to notice everything on the date. Were you hosted in a nice location or were you in a motel frequented by addicts and prostitutes?. Were there any concerns for special treatment? Did they consider your family? Were they stingy? Did they seem appreciative? Do the church members seem to like each other? Did your children connect? Were there children there the age of your children? In premarital counseling, the task is not to tell a couple to marry or not to marry. When discussing marriage, I tell the unmarried, "You should not marry someone until you know why you should not marry them!" Do not get me wrong. I love me! However, there are some things about me that I don't even like. To suggest you want to marry someone and you love everything about them suggests you don't know them very well. Likewise, in evaluating a congregation, the purpose is to make sure you understand what the difficulties are going to be before you arrive. So you must consider: What do members around you say about this congregation? How did they transport you? Did they take good care of you and your family or did it cost you more than you received, and if so, why? Did they provide transportation for your family as well, or just you? Are they organized in how they conduct a basic worship service? Do they act like they can tolerate constructive criticism or are they offended that someone is not impressed with a lackadaisical approach to worship? Do they have any aspirations for their future? Are there any specific goals they have in mind and are they open to yours? What assets do they have and do they have any idea or plans to implement along with those assets? In addition, a one-day date is usually not enough to evaluate a relationship. It is, therefore, critical to plan to spend several days with the group. This can be done by offering to conduct a mini-meeting, workshop or be a part of a weekend program. The point is that you will need some time to see them in more natural surroundings, and they need time to see you in the same light. A one-day, two-sermon visit may move you to a place that you will need to leave before you finish unpacking your bags.

CHURCH HISTORY

In addition, if you do not want to be bouncing around in your ministry for decades, you need to learn and research the congregation's history. How long do they retain preachers? Why do they think the last preacher left? Do they plan to have a contract? How dependable has their word been in the past? Why did the last preacher say he left? What does the last preacher think about this church and how much of what he says is fueled by other frustrations? What does the last preacher think the greatest challenges were? Will they provide housing? Do they expect you to live in their housing indefinitely? Will they assist you in the purchase of a home after a number of years? If the last preacher had a long-term ministry and was well loved, this may become an interim ministry unless you can establish your own clear identity apart from the former preacher.

Just like members talk about preachers, preachers talk about congregations. We have heard about the ones who are generous and the ones who don't mind seeing your family struggle to survive. We have heard about the ones who always war with every preacher, strongly dislike his children, quarrel with his wife, play hide-the-preachers-check, disrespect his gifts and think preaching is no more important than being the janitor. When the discussions come up, preachers often already know the name of the members who will be the biggest challenge at that location before they even meet the member personally. Unfortunately, there is often a great deal of truth about the Diotrepheus (3 John 9) in certain congregations. Just like John dropped a name, present day preachers drop names too.

LONGEVITY

You need to know the longevity of the preacher at this location. Normal is whatever you are accustomed to experiencing. A church that is not accustomed to having a preacher longer than two to five years can naturally begin to get edgy and change its mood when that normal time period has come. There is normally a good reason for good men to leave a location. It's a sign of advance research wisdom. Likewise, a congregation that has had a preacher for over twenty-five years will be comfortable with a long-term relationship. However, a church may change its response to a man if he is there longer than their normal experience. This suggests that his personality and gifts have impacted them and they are open to changes in their norm.

HOW TO EVALUATE PREACHERS
(THE PEW)

How is a church to evaluate a preacher? Every preacher is different. It is important that a congregation understands its emphasis and the emphasis of the man who preaches at their location. Every preacher is different. When a church is looking for a preacher, there are several areas they need to consider:

MIRROR

A congregation may bring a man in based on his education, message and chemistry. However, the reason they ask him to leave has to do with a long list of other issues. If we keep bringing in potential preachers based on how their speech and chemistry and want them to leave because they were not friendly, ineffective, not busy enough, not evangelistic, uncooperative, mean spirited, lack vision, disconnected, family problems or another whole list of issues, then we will continue the cycle. It has been said that a sign of insanity is to do the same thing, the same way expecting different results. Look at the preachers who have ministered to this church before. You need to answer honestly, why did they leave? If the church cannot see the part it played in the problem, then it cannot see the part it can play in the solution. It's always easier to make the departing preacher the scapegoat for a laundry list of church issues.

If you want or need a Pee Wee Herman preacher, don't date/interview Rambos! Understand yourself as a congregation and how your history has shaped you. Did you come into existence from a split? Do you do your best as a group if you are fighting some outside entity besides the devil? When did you function at your best and what were those conditions?

Many churches have not considered the preacher's own special emphasis and background. They have not considered if they are an Undertaker, Caretaker or Risk-takers. They have not considered if his "Philosophy of Ministry" fits theirs because they are not aware of their own "Philosophy of Ministry."

Before the preacher search begins, a church needs to sit down and look in the mirror. I have tried to keep a journal for a number of years so that I can better understand me. Each person needs to understand self before they can improve self. If I am out of shape, I need to understand my condition before I will be motivated to go to the gym. If a group is not honest about who they are perceived and how they seem to function then they can't experience healthy change. In conjunction, if a person cannot see the part they play in the problem, they will not be able to see the part they can play in the solution. If a church thinks the problem is every preacher and can't see that there may be leadership issues, moral issues, and non-spiritual attitudes among them, they will recreate the same set of problems and will not have real improvement. In other words, if a church keeps on doing the same things in the same way, they will keep getting the same results. Some of the same questions asked of self before dating again are the same questions that should be asked before a church scouts for a preacher. Some valid questions are: Who are you as a congregation? What are your strengths? What are your weaknesses? How many preachers have you had? What is the normal regularity of rotation of preachers from your location? What part did you play as a group in their leaving? What did you dislike about the preachers that have left? Why did you not see that characteristic before you brought them in? Were there signs that you overlooked that you should have seen? What is the perception of you as a group?

PREACHER'S STYLE

The story is told of a church that was looking for a preacher. They finally narrowed it down to two men. The church picked one of them to become their preacher. Both men came in and preached on a Sunday. They both used the same text and expressed the same emphasis. Someone asked a member, "How could you pick a preacher when they basically used the same text and the same emphasis?" The member said, "Both men preached about the importance of being saved and how anyone who is not saved would end up in hell. One preacher preached about it like it broke his heart, the other preached about it like he was glad they were going to hell. We chose the one with the broken heart!

The word of God cannot change and should not be changed. However, you can give ten preachers the same passage and they may not misinterpret or misuse the text, but you can still have ten sermons from ten different emphasis based on the mentality, research and personality of the preacher. 70%-90% of communication is nonverbal. This means most of what we say is not bound in the words which we use, but are instead in the way we use them. Voice tone and body language speaks volumes. Therefore, you cannot interpret every message from every preacher to be the same. It comes out of the intent of his heart. Jeremiah said *"9 But if I say, I will not mention him or speak any more in his name, "his word is in my heart like a fire, a fire shut up in my bones. I am weary of holding it in; indeed, I cannot."* Jeremiah was not bragging. Jeremiah wanted to quit! He only had two sermons. He had one sermon on death and another on destruction, so he only preached death and destruction. He did not focus on preaching good tidings of things to come. Isaiah was given a ministry of failure. God asked a fundamental question:

> *Isa. 6:8-10 Then I heard the voice of the Lord saying, "Whom shall I send? And who will go for us?" And I said, "Here am I. Send me!" 9 He said, "Go and tell this people: "Be ever hearing, but never understanding; be ever seeing, but never perceiving.' 10 Make the heart of this people calloused; make their ears dull and close their eyes. Otherwise they might see with their eyes, hear with their ears, understand with their hearts, and turn and be healed." 11 Then I said, "For how long, O Lord?"*

God told Isaiah his ministry would consist of preaching to a people who will not understand or change. Isaiah wanted to know how long he would preach to people who would not change. These two men were called to deliver messages of hope for future generations. Jonah preached one message with a bad attitude and it changed a whole city. Noah preached a lifetime and only convinced his family. Believing your audience will never change will change the way you communicate to them.

PREACHER'S THEOLOGY

What are the core beliefs of this preacher? The key is to find out as much as you can about what the minister believes before there is an interview, and at the interview, identify what are the important issues for your congregation. Be careful to keep major doctrine the main focus. Every battleground is not worth fighting over. Decide what the really important issues are that impact where you live and try not to major in the minors.

PREACHER'S FAMILY

One of the most important things a married minister brings to a congregation is his family. If he is married, the church needs to be concerned about the health of his marriage. There are no perfect marriages. However, it is good if they at least like each other. What is his family like? Is it important to you that his family feels connected? A disconnected, unhappy, disturbed family is going to have an impact on your congregation. It's not that you are employing his family or expecting anything specific out of them, but it is the case that you want to know will they be able to assimilate into your congregational environment. If they cannot connect and assimilate it is going to become a problem later when members begin to feel a disconnection because this new family does not seem to want to bond with them. A strong family value modeled by the church's public leader can be a powerful influence in your community and church. Therefore, before committing to the preacher, take time to get to know the spouse and family. Spend enough time with them so you have a good sense of how they relate to one another.

PREACHER'S FINANCES

For many preachers, the move to another church is a chance for financial improvement for their family. Unfortunately, most preachers know that the best raise you will typically get is the one that comes when you move. For this reason, many are already struggling before they talk with a church. Many congregations still operate under the idea of "Lord you keep him humble and we will keep him poor" philosophy. So I am not saying every preacher should have excellent credit and be sitting on a huge bank account. However, it is important to have some idea whether this family is able to meet basic living expenses every other month and are not being evicted every six months for nonpayment of rent. Ask questions about the candidate's finances and don't apologize for it. If you hire a minister who is heavily in debt, your church may eventually suffer for it. Is he a preacher who will be asking for an advance every week? Does he know or can he learn how to manage his finances? I'm not suggesting this is to be done for the sake of discounting a man; in many cases, they have not learned or been taught how to manage money. Identify if they are open or willing to learn how to manage their funds. Plan to treat them like family. If a man's credit is bad and he can't manage his finances, how is he going to emphasize good stewardship? In conjunction, congregations need to get away from the "what is the least we can get you here for?" mentality. Don't start asking questions about funds if at the end of the day you are only offering starvation wages. Try to come to a financial agreement his family can live on.

INTEGRITY

Every church deserves a minister with *integrity*. Because a man preaches from the Bible does not mean he has conquered every sin and battle in the Bible. He is a member of the church as well. He has struggles just like everyone else. Ask the candidate about his struggles, addictions, or other immoral activities. Ask the candidate's references, and then check with people who know the candidate, but weren't included in his list of references. The question needs to be asked regardless of the candidates desire to be this open. These things should always be done in a spirit of caring and love that shows your concern is for all men and especially those of the household of faith. Do not start shooting our wounded preachers. Peter was better able to strengthen the brethren because of his fall. So, do not hold a mistake against a man for life.

If your church is seriously considering hiring a person as minister, then the candidate's past and current churches or ministries should be called. This should only be done with the potential minister's permission, but it must be done. The local church deserves to know the answer to these questions. It is a huge mistake to ignore them. Someone should also visit the church where he is. You need to see him in his natural environment. Be aware that where he goes will be like where he came from after the same period of time.

LEADERSHIP AND PERSONALITY

The *preacher's leadership and personality needs to* match the needs of the congregation. Leaders should consider what kind of minister the church needs. Does the congregation need strong visionary leadership? Is dynamic preaching really the only need? Is sensitive pastoral care important at the church? Will a mean-spirited preacher work best here? First, understand self before trying to understand others. Do not expect a bull of a man to be gentle.

THE PROCESS

The following characteristics are important for the process:

- *Pray.* Ask God into every component of your search. Don't just say it, practice it.

- *Be Direct.* Look out and determine based on preachers you know, who fits the kind of qualities you want. Talk to them and consider them. Even if they are not available, it allows you to focus on the type of candidate you want.

- *Systematic.* Create as objective a process as possible and try to hold each man to the same basic procedures. Take the time to develop a good system.

- *Get Ready to Date.* Plan to use your resources to properly pay for serious candidates to come in and spend the time examining your potential to fit together.

- *Be Introspective.* Discuss honestly what your church personality is, and what you think needs to happen for it to become be more like Jesus.

Please take this important task seriously. Your church deserves to be well-led. God expects His church to be well led. Your community and the lost, hurting people in it deserve your church to be well led.

Larry Ivery Sr.

Larry Ivery Sr. was born and raised in Dayton, Ohio. Presently, he resides in Henderson, Tennessee with his wife. He is married to Dianne (Pope) for thirty-three years. Their children are Tony (thirty-two), Teneal (twenty-nine) of Kane Ridge, Tennessee, and TaKeisha (twenty-three).

Ivery Graduated from Oklahoma Christian with a BS in Bible; Freed Hardeman University with both the Masters of Ministry and Master of Science in Counseling degrees, and Luther Rice University with a Doctor of Ministry Degree.

He has preached in small Church ministry for the past thirty-one years. He served the Thompson Street congregation in Lepanto, Arkansas for four years and the Oak Grove Church of Christ in Henderson, Tennessee for nineteen years. Presently, he has served the Church of Christ @ Church Street for the past eight years. Presently, he serves as one of the elders for the congregation as well as serving as the Executive Director for the Tennessee Children's Home, a residential treatment program in Tennessee. Dr. Ivery has conducted various workshops and Gospel meetings in twenty-one states, Japan, Jamaica, Germany, and Brazil.

CHAPTER 6

The Validity of the Small Church

Larry Ivery Sr.

—ന—

Here in the United States of America, the present religious community has made some rapid changes in the concepts pertaining to Church size. In the 1970's and 1980's, greater emphasis was placed on the size of the Church. Many began to look at the large Church as means of accomplishing God's will for America. Although numerous, the small Church became the less desired of the Churches in the urban setting. Large is associated with better in so many people's eyes. Is bigger necessarily better? Or is smaller necessarily not as good?

It is stated that two-thirds of the Churches in the United States and Canada average less than 120 in Sunday morning worship service. At least one half of all protestant congregations in North America can be labeled "small."

What is small when it applies to Churches? Churches have been small. Before urbanization, industrialization, and centralization, 150 would have been considered more than ample. In fact, in some geographical areas a congregation of a hundred is considered large. It certainly depends on the area of location. However, generally, the thinking is that anything under 150 is too small.

If a small congregation grows into a medium or large congregation, it will not be the same congregation. Each congregation is different from one another. A small Church that becomes large is not the same and in the same vein a large, when it begins to decline, is not the same Church.

Years ago, I listened to a speaker as he discussed the eldership of the congregation he served for the past thirty-five years; he shared some profound insights into Church growth and leadership development. He made the statement that the elders that served when he began with that congregation, although good and able men for that time could not serve the congregation that existed that day. That made good sense.

Many small rural African American congregations have less than one hundred members in attendance on Sunday mornings, and on Sunday and Wednesday evenings, the attendance is usually sixty or less. The above information may be slightly inflated because according to Mac Lynn's compiled data, thirty congregations in seventeen towns in both west and middle Tennessee averaged forty-eight in attendance on Sunday mornings.

The general attitude is that there is something wrong with the small Church. Presently, young men who are aspiring to be ministers, once they complete their education, look for the larger congregations to serve. Their desire is to be ministers of the Word, but not ministers of God. Other seasoned ministers see a man who is working with a small congregation as an inadequate servant of God. Many believe that the larger the congregation, the healthier. We have all types of bodies in this world. Some are taller, wider, shorter, and thinner and their health is based on their size. Rather, their health is based on genetics and health practices. So it is with the Church. Its health has less to do with its size, rather the size and health of the original dream and its health practices.

IS THE SMALL CHURCH REALLY VALID?

While there are many small Churches that will close their doors this year, sixty percent of the congregations in North America will not. Most of these congregations are not going to get to the golden number of one hundred fifty; they will remain relatively small. Does this mean that the small Church is not valid? No! It does not mean that at all. Therefore, a pertinent question to ask is what are the strengths and weaknesses of the small Church?

There are several strengths that may be discussed regarding the small Church. The first is that the small Church emphasizes relationships. The parallel is to the family. In the small Church, God is the Father, Christ is the Bridegroom, the Church is the bride, and all who obey the gospel are children. Have you ever noticed that many large congregations are going to small group ministries? One of the reasons for this is because they lack the relational aspect of the family. This is natural with the small Church. In the small congregation people are known by their name. I was once told by a ministry-minister in a twenty-six thousand member Baptist Church that he desired to meet and talk with his pastor. He had never met him!

The small Church is resilient and persistent. I spoke with a woman who described the congregation where her father-in-law had preached several years ago as being resilient. She did not use the word resilient, but her description of the congregation certainly described the concept. This congregation has an annual program which draws several of the former members who have left that area, back for the occasion. She says the building is exactly the same, and although there is the same number of members attending (50), they are not the same members. It appears to have weathered a great number of storms.

WEAKNESSES OF THE SMALL CHURCH

Small Churches have difficulty growing because they have inadequate financial resources. There are five areas that are affected by the lack of financial resources: The first is an inadequate education program. Second, the education program does not only lack adequate funding but generally there are not enough teachers to man the program properly. Third, the worship may not have enough men to effectively work the worship period and because of a lack of funding the congregation may not be able to have an effective benevolence program. Additionally, small African American congregations are very rarely involved in the support of missions and do not have full-time ministers.

Another area is that there is usually a limited number in the population to draw from. This impacts the evangelistic program negatively. Even if the funding is there, people are not as excited about doing evangelism.

Willimon and Wilson claim that "finances are a perennial problem." The small congregation tends to spend a large proportion of its income (often between one-half and two-thirds) for the minister to serve. This problem is complimented by another problem. Although the congregation is spending a significant amount of their resources on the minister, it is still not enough to support his needs. The minister often must be employed in secular work to provide adequately for himself and his family.

Another weakness is that there is a wall between the insiders and outsiders. This wall is the membership circle and the fellowship circle. It is an exclusionary atmosphere and while it does not fit every congregation perfectly, it exists in the small Church. A small Church like a large Church may be cliquish.

CAN THE SMALL CHURCH BE VITAL?

The small Church can be vital in its worship. Willimon and Wilson state, "There may be small Churches without a building, without an educational program, without a budget, and without formal organizational structure, but there are no small Churches without preaching and worship." Of course, not all small Churches are carrying on satisfactory worship programs, but that does not detract from the fact that worship is central in the life and experience of every Church.

Some had identified three adjectives that describe effective worship in the small Church: First, worship is important. It is this writer's experience with the small Church that people will attend the a.m. worship and miss the Bible study. There is the worship crowd which consists of people who are faithful in attendance to the worship services. Even if the worship is conducted before the Bible studies, people will worship and leave. It is very difficult to get full cooperation in attendance matters in the small Church, where it seems that it would be possible to accomplish.

Second, it is indigenous. People who are faithful are usually loyal. You can count on the same people to attend. There are some who will get there on time and others who are late at the exact same time week after week, but they will be at the worship.

Third, it is inclusive. The small Church welcomes everyone to worship. There is no separation of children and youth from the assembly. Everyone is in the auditorium during the worship period. Visitors are welcomed and the same enthusiasm that is expressed when no visitors are present is expressed when visitors are present.

The small Church can be vital in its preaching. The minister in the small Church is a servant of the Word. The significance of variety and relevance in the small Churches of the Word to life is evident. The preaching is not based on showmanship and the size of the crowd. Although the minister will more than likely be less educated, less charismatic, and less of an administrator, he will be experienced and personable. He will preach with conviction and power and the congregation will be blessed as a result.

In conclusion, the small Church is a vital cog in our life and work here in the United States of America. If forced, even those who do not like Church would prefer a small Church over a mega-church. The Church can grow, but the question that begs to be answered is, "How does God want it to grow?"

Ervin C. Jackson

Ervin C. Jackson received his bachelors of Arts in Biblical Studies from Heritage Christian University in the spring of 1993. He then completed a Masters of Arts degree in New Testament Studies at Freed Hardeman University and a second MA in Higher Education Administration from the University of Alabama. Continuing his educational pursuits, Jackson earned an Interdisciplinary PhD in Organizational Leadership at the University of Alabama. His dissertation investigated the impact of diverse-team transformational leadership on the culture of an historically African American Church of Christ. Over the years, Jackson has served as an Associate Professor of Church Leadership, the Dean of Students at Heritage Christian, the Dean of the School of Business and Leadership and as Associate Professor of Leadership Studies at Amridge University. Jackson now serves as the pulpit minister of the Hartman Road Church of Christ and teaches Public Speaking as well as Voice and Diction at Eastern Florida State College. He has preached throughout the United States and has performed mission work in the Ukraine, Mexico, Guatemala, Peru, and Africa. He has published various articles in numerous brotherhood publications, speaks on brotherhood lectureships, as well as conducts leadership workshops and gospel meetings.

CHAPTER 7

Can We Blend?

Ervin C. Jackson

—ɯ—

Can we blend? This is a question we need to ask ourselves as
Christians. The question is one that assesses our potential or
ability. Do we as disciples of Jesus Christ have the ability to come
together and worship in the same place? Is it possible for us to
discard the things that have caused our divisions, to come together
in one place as one people? I'm using the term "blend" metaphori-
cally to prompt you as the reader to visualize several ingredients
being mixed together in one container to form something that is
qualitatively different and unique from that which it began. In the
process of making a cake, one blends eggs, flour, sugar, butter, and
milk together to produce something that is qualitatively different
from the individual ingredients. So the question, "Can we blend,"
evaluates if we as Christians: white Christians, black Christians,
Hispanic Christians, Japanese Christians, and Chinese Christians
have the ability to come together as one.

Although we have cultural differences, I believe that we are
qualitatively the same. The ingredients of a cake are qualitatively

101

different; nevertheless, they can be blended in one bowl to form something that is both tasty and delightful for all to partake. I'm not referring to things that are qualitatively different; I'm referring to things that are qualitatively the same. I'm referring to people who basically have the same type of feelings, personalities, dreams, and goals; people who share in a desire to care for their families, and those who desire to make it to heaven. The Bible teaches us that we have the same origin. Many times this is something that Christian's fail to recognize; however, it is true that we all came from Adam and Eve. The Bible tells us that Eve is the mother of all that lives. Therefore, the question is relevant. Can we blend? Do we have the potential and ability as Christians to come together and worship in the same place?

In answering that question, we must first look at reality. Several decades ago Martin Luther King Jr., adequately described the state of American religion in his speech entitled "Remaining Awake Through a Great Revolution," delivered at the National Cathedral in Washington, D.C., on March 31, 1968. King said, "[W]e must face the sad fact that eleven o'clock on Sunday morning when we stand to sing, 'In Christ , there is no east nor west,' we stand in the most segregated hour of America" (Carson & Holloran, 1998). Dr. King said that about forty-five years ago, but in forty-five years we still languor in the same condition. It continues to remain the most segregated hour in America today. But why is that so? Why are there Black churches and White churches? Why are there Hispanic congregations and congregations of different nationalities of people? If we are all qualitatively the same, and are worshipping the same God, then what necessitates that we have to be divided? The problem this question addresses is intensified when we notice the practices of our secular world.

It is obvious that blending occurs every day in the secular world. In secular society there is blending in schools, restaurants, and we live in the same neighborhoods. In Alabama, I lived in a neighborhood with a White neighbor on one side, a Chinese family on the other, a biracial relationship (White and Hispanic) immediately across the street, and I am black. If we can live like that in a community, why can't we get together in the church? Societally, our marriages show the evidence of blending. People are coming together disregarding their ancestries and families are mixing. In a special issue of *Newsweek* magazine entitled "Redefining Race in America," they argued for the redefinition of race in America, because the notion of race is changing. They argued that the face of America is now very different as opposed to years ago. In America, we now have Trinidadian Sicilians, we have families where the father is Chinese-Irish-French-German-Swedish and the wife is Italian-Irish-Japanese. The article showed people who were German-Jewish-Korean and others who were African-American Trinidadian. The face of America is changing; therefore, if the church is to be effective in outreach and yet continues our segregated practices, where are all these different people going to go to church? Will we establish churches for each special blend of ethnicity?

Spiritual Constraints

Why have we not blended? Are we hindered by spiritual constraints? Do spiritual constraints dictate that we should not get together? According to John 17:20-ff, Jesus prayed not only for His disciples, but He prayed for everyone who believes in Him through the words His disciples would speak. Therefore, the intention He communicated in that prayer was that they all would be one. That oneness was to be qualitatively similar to the oneness Jesus had with the Father. He said that the outcome of that oneness would be that the entire world would know that Jesus was sent by God. Therefore, among some of Jesus' last words were words expecting that His believers would pursue unity.

In Ephesians 2:1-19, we learn that we are to be fellow citizens of the same body. "Same" is not an ambiguous concept. We know that means one. In John 13:13, we are commanded to love one another. He says the extent of that love should be to the same measure as His love for us. Jesus loved us so much that He gave Himself not only for the black man or the white man, He died for everybody. This same love functions to challenge every disciple in this modern age. Are we hindered to come together by spiritual constraints? Act 17:26 says that we are one blood, Galatians 3:28 tells us that there is no more bond, free, male, female, black, white, etc.; but we are all one in Christ Jesus. So it is safe to conclude that it is not spiritual constraints that keep us apart. For spiritual insight into the word of God communicates the unmistakable message of human togetherness. So why have we not blended? I believe that our problem is not rooted in spiritual prohibitions given by God, but rather in the culture accepted by humans.

Social Constraints

Most people would rather stay apart from others that they perceive to be different. Culture is a major contributor to the differences experienced in people. Edgar Schein defined culture as:

A pattern of basic assumptions invented, discovered or developed by a given group as it learns to cope with its problems of external adaptation and internal integration that has worked well enough to be considered valid, and therefore, to be taught to new members as the correct way to perceive, think, feel in relation to those problems.

Schein is saying the one group learns to deal with a problem in certain ways and passes it on to others in their social group. Another group may have the same problems, but learns to deal with them differently because they are separate from the other group. As my group learns to deal with a problem in a certain way, it becomes the way of the folk. As it becomes the way of the folk or "folkways," then I tend to behave that way consistently as well as those associated with my group. Now if you are not meeting with my group, your group will learn different ways of interacting. Therefore, when we try to come together, your group's folkways are different from my group's folkways.

I have spoken Spanish for the past fifteen-years, and over the years I have learned that some Spanish phrases must be expressed in ways that don't make sense when stated in English the same way. When I was learning, one of my Spanish-speaking friends from Mexico explained to me that when you learn Spanish, you are learning Spanish culture as well. He said, "You have to learn to say it the way we say it." So as I learned Spanish, I had to learn to say things differently from the way I say things in my group. That was difficult for me; nevertheless, I understood that because they were from Mexico, they have learned certain ways of expressing ideas that works well for them, and since the group from which I acquired language was not from Mexico, we have learned a different way that works well for us. Neither language is better than the other because they both have the potential to communicate the same ideas. So language and culture can present a problem that can hinder togetherness; but people overcome linguistic and cultural barriers every day. So again I ask the question, why have we not blended?

Is it also because of socialization? Upon entering this world, we immediately begin the process of being socialized. We begin learning how to act in social settings. We learn how to worship: some a little louder than others, while some prefer quiet worship. Others may be more excited in worship while others may be more solemn than others. We learn many of these behaviors from our parents and peer groups. Socialization has caused us to do things differently. When two groups are apart from each other, they are naturally going to learn to do things differently. How do groups learn to do things the same way? They have to come together. When they come together they must have the attitude that my way is not higher than your way, neither is your way higher than my way. These differing groups have to learn to work together to accomplish unity.

There is a principle that many church sociologist mention that is related to church growth. They reference it as the Homogeneous Unit Principle. They say that churches tend not to grow when churches are made up of people of differing ethnicity. The reason for this assumption is because men like to become Christians without crossing barriers. The reason people don't like to cross race barriers is because we don't like to feel uncomfortable. We don't like to cross financial, economic, or educational status barriers because it makes us feel uncomfortable. I think McGavran's Homogeneous Unit Principle is archaic in view of the ethnic advances we have made in our society; nevertheless, even this principle recognizes that the problem does not rest in biblical prescription, but rather in human preference.

The problem is "we don't like." But the problem within what we don't like is "I." "I" is also that which stands in the middle of sin. Paul says that we have a sinful nature. He says that our nature causes us to do what we want to do. The reason Eve sinned in the beginning was because Eve wanted to become knowledgeable like God. She had an "I" problem. She wanted to have more than what God wanted for her. Her "I" got in the way causing her to fail. We have to watch out for "I" because it keeps us from growing and doing what God intends. If Jesus had an "I" problem, He would have never come to this earth. He loved the world so much that He gave His life for us. He didn't have an "I" problem because He was willing to give the best gift that has ever been given, and that is the gift of Himself. Philippians 2 says that He humbled Himself. He didn't think being equal with God was something to grasp at, but instead He humbled Himself and lowered Himself to take on the form of a servant. Paul says, we ought to arm our self with the same mentality. We have to be willing to humble ourselves and learn to serve one another. When we begin to serve one another, God will receive the glory. We will stop dividing ourselves and see ourselves accomplishing what God has called us to carry out from the beginning. We know God wants us to be one and we have to agree that the potential to blend exists. Therefore, if there is failure, it resides in human weakness. Failure to blend is because we are weak and unwilling to deal with difference.

If we succeed in blending, it will be because of divine accomplishment. Success will be because God has empowered us to have the ability to succeed. If we succeed, we have learned the mind-set of God and we have learned how to love our neighbor as ourselves. Jesus, when asked the question, "Who is my neighbor?" told the story about a Samaritan who encountered a Jew who had been robbed and beaten. Other Jews had passed by this fallen Jew, but no one stopped to help him because they all had "I" problems. But Jesus said a Samaritan man who was despised and disliked by the Jews stopped to help this man. The Samaritan didn't care that the Jew didn't like him but still saw to taking care of his needs. If we develop that same attitude, we will then begin to experience the fullness of God.

I conducted a research project in the Memphis area a few years ago by examining by survey four churches consisting of a variety of ethnic make ups. One church was African-American, another was Caucasian. The third congregation was approximately half Caucasian and half African-American. The last church was predominantly African-American with a 10% Caucasian mix. I examined their worship styles, their frequency of racial interaction, their attitudes toward social integration, their attitudes toward diverse leadership, and finally their attitudes toward internal diversity. My findings were that the hidden culture of a church consisting of more than one ethnic group was significantly different from the cultures of churches consisting of one group. White churches and Black churches were more alike than the church consisting of a significant population of White and Black Christians. My findings suggested that the more a congregation consisted of one group, there would be a greater tendency for the presence of prejudice within that group. So if a person wants to maintain a racist attitude, they would most likely worship in a place where everyone is ethnically like them. If an individual wants to harbor hatred and continue to discriminate against other ethnicities, they will be found in a group of people who are not diverse.

In my seventh year of being the senior minister of my first full-time work, I told the congregation that if this congregation wants to continue being predominantly African-American, I would not feel comfortable remaining in their fellowship. I had grown to the point where God had helped me to recognize that we must learn to forgive all humans, and love everyone. So how can I say "I love you" and not have any fellowship with you. Another thing found from the Memphis study is that the more a congregation consists of more than one group, the greater potential exists for evangelizing across color lines. It is easier for an African-American to successfully bring a visitor who is Caucasian when the church has a healthy representation of both groups. It will be more diffi-cult for an African-American to bring a Caucasian visitor if they believe they will be the only Caucasians in the audience. It will be difficult for disciples to evangelize their neighbors who live in their same neighborhood if the church has no one representing the group of your potential visitor. Therefore, because we remain separated ethnically, we limit the amount of evangelism that can be done. But is God pleased? God wants us to reach all men. Color lines should not exist.

My study led me to conclude that churches consisting of one ethnic group can never completely experience the fullness of God's presence exemplified in spiritual love and exhibited through human interaction. Ephesians 2:11-21 and Ephesians 3:14-21 tells us when we begin to come together, we learn love. Humanity does not really understand love. We don't understand the capacity to give our son for someone else as God did. We only experiment with love. The way we learn about love is through interacting with people who are not like ourselves. We learn how to love when we can continue to interact with and appreciate someone with whom we have conflict. Most couples learn more about love once they get married and start living in the same household. Before a couple gets married, their perspective is idealistically challenged so that it seems that their partner can do no wrong. However, once they are married, time teaches them that they have many differences and they must learn to accept some things that they may not like about their partner. After a while they will have children who will run through the house doing things that the couple will not appreciate, like breaking things and tearing things. Nevertheless, no matter how many negative things the children do, the couple will not throw them out because the children are theirs. This unit made up of husband, wife and children are family and cannot allow conflict or differences to divide them from one another. The more they commit as family to learn to appreciate one another and their differences, the more they understand and put into practice the concept of love.

Love keeps people together. A church that consists of one group can only learn to appreciate the differences of people who look just like them. What more are we doing than the heathen, when we only love our own? The heathen will love and take care of theirs, so how do we go beyond? How do we love someone different from those we consider our own? How do we experience a greater love? God didn't care what we looked like; He was willing to die for every human regardless of ethnicity. What concerns me is that the secular world appears to be more committed to diversity than the church. That's a problem! Recently, I was reading a Chrysler advertisement that said, "Diversity is just a noun unless you do something about it." It appears that everybody in the secular world is talking about diversity, but the question is, "who is moving toward it?"

In the 1950s, with Brown v. Board of Education, the government forced schools to integrate by imposing sanctions; but in my opinion, the church should have been leading the way by making efforts to integrate their own worship assemblies and being an example to society at large. The government successfully integrated the schools; however, the only institution the government could not integrate is still segregated. That is the church. Separation of church and state limited the government from being able to sanction the church; but the will of God still calls the church to accountability. Jesus said, "My sheep hear My voice." Ephesians 2 says, "...we are no more foreigners, but fellow citizens, built together so that God can inhabit us through His Spirit." So the question is, "What should we do?"

I believe God's people ought to be moving toward diversity. God's people ought to be trying to grow more spiritual. The more spiritual one becomes, the more that person will recognize the body of this bondage (our fleshly self) and its impediments. We understand that focus on skin color is unimportant and immature. We need to understand the higher existence within everyone and that is the spiritual being.

"There is therefore no condemnation to them who walk not after the flesh but after the Spirit" (Romans 8:1). When will we truly walk after the Spirit? When will we get to the place where we can love a White person just as much as we love Black people or love Hispanic people just as much as we love others? When will we get to the point where we can walk and talk and fellowship and interact and have no problem? When can we get there? I think the answer lies in self-denial and following Christ unconditionally.

James Jones Jr.

James Jones Jr. holds two doctorate degrees, a doctorate of Theology ThD and a PhD in philosophy of Psychology. Successfully completed the South Carolina Commission on Alcohol and Drug Abuse Management Institute, Certified Addictions Counselor, completed the Southeastern School of Alcohol and Other Drugs at the University of Georgia for strategies and techniques for employee assistance programs. Has worked as a Division Director for the Aiken, SC, Alcohol and Drug Abuse Center. Worked as Director of the Durham, NC, Methadone Treatment Center; Chaplain at Manning Correctional Institution in Columbia, SC, Director of Pastoral Training School in Augusta, GA. and minister of churches of Christ in North Carolina, South Carolina, Georgia and presently in El Paso, TX at the Montwood Church of Christ.

CHAPTER 8

Identifying the Church by Its Organizational Structure: Elders, Deacons, and Preachers

James Jones Jr.

—m—

CONTENTS

Introduction

When the church was established in Jerusalem, according to Acts chapter 2, it grew in number by the grace of God. It grew with daily additions of men, women and children. Acts 5:14 states "And believers were increasingly added to the Lord, multitudes of both men and women."

God, of course, had an organizational structure already in mind. That plan for the church was in the mind of God before the world was made (Ephesians 3:9-11). Of course, God already had an organization structure in mind for the church before the world was made (Ephesians 3:9-11). As churches were established, the scriptures teach that elders were appointed in every city (Acts 14:23). It is the minister's job to appoint elders according to Titus 1:5-9. We must not move away from that responsibility.

Can a congregation have deacons without having elders? Yes, it can. Such was the case of the Jerusalem church at first (Acts 6:1-7). But each congregation must work to develop elders because they are tasked with the job of overseeing the local church. We must not be satisfied with a minister only or minister and deacon structure in a congregation because that is not the organizational structure of the church in scripture. Congregations are to be locally organized with elders, deacons, ministers, and teachers (Ephesians 4:10-16). Therefore, in this chapter, we will discuss some leadership in general issues, relationships between elders and preachers in their working agreements, and about deacons. Elders oversee the congregation, including the preacher. And they must work together with mutual respect and service to God. Between elders and ministers, let us stop arguing over who is over whom. The Bible specifically says elders oversee the church (Acts 20:28-31). It never says that about ministers. Ministers are tasked with setting the church in order and appointing elders, (Titus 1:5-9) which is a tremendous task. The Bible teaches that elders have a specific job of overseeing the flock and ministers have a specific job of preaching the word and insuring that the church is consistently complying with the word of God. Deacons have a ministry of service, which is essential in the wellbeing of the care of the church. If each operates within its area of responsibility, there should be no conflict. If a conflict develops, can it not be resolved as other conflicts are resolved by the plain teaching of the scriptures? If we, as ministers, have our jobs placed on the line because appointed elders have been consumed with power rather than purpose, that is an issue between them and God and God will always take care of us.

The Need for Strengthening Power

The word of God teaches us that we are in a spiritual warfare. Eph. 6:10-20; our mission is spiritual (Mark 16:15-16). Leaders themselves need to be strengthened and led by God.

1. God's leaders need to be men of prayer.

2. Men that handle right the word of God – 2 Tim. 2:15.

3. Men that are empowered by the Spirit of God – Eph. 1:19; Rom. 4:17.

A clear example of leadership is seen in the life and work of Nehemiah. Nehemiah was touched by the need of his people. Chapter 1:4 "... sat down and wept and mourned ... and I was fasting and praying before the God of heaven."

In verses 4 through 11, there are four very significant factors revealed that are true in the lives of competent spiritual leaders.

1. A leader has a clear recognition of the needs. Sometimes there are people in responsible leadership positions who never seem to see the problems they ought to be solving. Nehemiah was not preoccupied with his own agenda. Sometimes leaders are so preoccupied with their personal agendas that they don't hear the needs of those they serve, and cannot 'see' where God's people need to go.

2. A leader needs to be personally concerned with the needs. Nehemiah was called to build the wall, but first he wept over the ruins. Nehemiah fasted and prayed. He demonstrated personal concern. Sometimes leaders want recognition but not the involvement.

3. The mark of a serious leader is he goes first to God with the problem. The challenges we have in life will not be solved until we take it to God in prayer. In verse 5, we hear Nehemiah say, "I beseech Thee, 0 Lord God of heaven..." He prayed. He even confirmed his part in the problem. Verses 6 and 7 "Let thine ear now be attentive and thine eyes open to hear the prayer of thy servant... Thy servants, confessing the sins of the sons of Israel ...I and my father's house have sinned..."

4. A leader makes himself available to meet the needs. Nehemiah recognized the need clearly. He got involved in it. He took it to God. Now he was available to meet the needs. A genuine leader is marked by diligent faithfulness is the midst of a task.

Spiritual Relationship between Elders and Preachers

Second Peter 1:5-7 teaches us the qualities that should exist in all Christians, therefore they must abound in elders and preachers.

1. Both elders and preachers should be men of faith. Committed, dedicated and diligent in their faithfulness to God. II Peter 1:3; Hebrews 11:6

2. Both elders and preachers must be virtuous men. In II Peter 1:5 "virtue" is manly, courageous servants of God.

3. Both elders and preachers must be knowledgeable men of service. II Timothy 2:15; II Peter 1:5

4. Both elders and preachers must be men that display self-control. Neither can be men that are out of control in any area of their life. II Peter 1:6: Titus 1:8

5. Both elders and preachers must have perseverance or endurance, the ability to hold on to their principals. II Peter 1:6; Proverbs 16:17

6. Both elders and preachers must be godly men. And those who practice godliness. II Peter 1:6; I Timothy 6:6

7. Both elders and preachers must possess brotherly kindness. II Peter 1:7; Hebrews 13:1

8. Both elders and preachers must be men that demonstrate love. II Peter 1:7; John 13:34-35

The Working Relationship of Elders and Preachers

A preacher is a servant of God and not a subordinate. Elders and preachers have been given different areas of responsibility by God to function in the church. Elders are to oversee the congregations and preachers are to preach and teach the gospel and to appoint elders (Titus 1:5-9). If there are existing elders at the congregation where he preaches, both elders and preachers are to function in their delegated area of responsibility with no wrangling over who is over whom. The elders are specially tasked with the job of overseeing the flock. A preacher is not just like every other member of the church. He has a specific task with leadership in preaching and training the church and evangelizing the community. He, the preacher, is a servant of the Lord and though his work is under the supervision of the elders in a local congregation, he is not subservient to them. The preacher is under no more obligation to his elders than they are obligated to him as colleagues in the business of saving souls and promoting the growth of the congregation they serve together. The major difference in their working conditions is that a full-time minister is devoting all his time to preaching the gospel of Christ, and answering daily the calls for help, which in substance, reflect the whole spectrum of human difficulty. Or if the minister has to sustain himself by working an additional job, along with serving the church, this brings its own set of additional challenges for the minister.

All details relative to their current program and future plans for development should be discussed by the elders with their preachers prior to beginning their work together. The elders and preachers should have an understanding from the beginning of the minister's contractual agreement regarding salary, raise, vacation, holiday leave, evangelistic meetings, lectureship, sick time, etc. All of this should be in writing for the benefit of all parties.

Participants in Business Meetings

All ministers and elders should regularly meet in business meetings. Since the aim of the business meeting is for planning the programs, work, and growth of their congregation, it is imperative that the minister, whose life's work is involved in these plans for operation must be included. Ministers and elders need to be equally informed of all phases of operational affairs and future plans of the church where they serve.

Since intelligence, education, wisdom, and an influential mind are the prerequisite of the eldership in employing a man to serve as their spiritual advisor, it is a lack of their own stability, by a contradiction of their own prerequisite requirements when elders shut the minister out of the business meetings.

Disagreements between Elders And Preachers

Human relations between preachers and elders may be termed equalitarian and in this respect, their relationship should be neither preacher-dominated nor elder-dominated. However, as in all relationships or business of close human contact there will be a difference in opinions at times, but these occasional differences need not be harmful, either to their harmonious unity or detrimental to their work. In fact, when human disagreements are recognized as the prerogative of personal thinking and discussed in the spirit of Christianity, with loving respect one for the other, such differences may prove to be a helpful stimulus for greater growth. When Christian attitude prevails in the hearts of both elders and preachers during these times of human opinions, their relationships can be strengthened in Christ.

When the preacher of this church knows of some work which needs to be done in the promotion of a better program for more growth, he has the freedom of expression. If the eldership does not agree with his suggestions, or visualize the need for this proposal being put into immediate effect, this preacher, with all due respect for their opinion, pursues one of two courses of action; he either presents an appeal for his suggestion, with all the pros and cons necessary to convince his elders for the reasons justifying the proposal or abides by their wisdom in rejecting the plan.

There is never any righteousness in the outcome of disagreements between elders and their preachers resulting in malicious resentfulness, since infrequent differences in opinion are a result of normal human minds and individual thinking. Extreme caution must always be exercised prayerfully, however, by all individual elders and preachers that un-Christian attitudes, and betraying self-righteous feelings, will not develop from a friendly disagreement within their groups. Since all men are human beings, there is the danger of malignancy being the ultimate reward for such pernicious attitudes and Christians are warned by the Lord to guard against having an evil disposition toward one another. Thus, frequent variances in human opinions between elders and preachers can tend to be injurious to each person involved, and indicative of uncharitable feeling among them. There is an appreciable difference between a Christian difference in opinion and maleficent quarreling.

Operational Freedom for the Preacher

The work of a minister is so diversified as to render incapable the possibility, in some instances, of maintaining strictly enforced

119

office hours without some flexibility. If a preacher is full time, I believe office time is necessary. There needs to be structure in every minister's schedule. That means some fixed hours that the congregation can reach him at the office or call him for visitation, counseling, Bible study, time for study, meditation, prayer, and etc. But he also must be free to do outreach, make himself community conscience and be familiar with the city. I believe that a minster must develop the confidence of the elders and congregation that when he is away from the office he is doing productive work to help the cause of Christ.

Preaching the gospel of Christ is the primary purpose of a preacher's life, but this soul saving effort is not confined to the pulpit only; it is divided into the many channels of response to human cries for help, with each one presenting a different form of opportunity. He stands, or falls, by his persuasive ability in the pulpit and long hours for study in preparation for acceptable presentation of his sermons and Bible study lessons. I believe that minister must develop disciplined time management for his life, whether he works from home or the office. In larger churches where there are paid staff, he must possess the skills to manage the staff effectively. His behavior, actions and personality must represent Christ at all times. He must respect elders, deacons, and the rest of the church in order to have the respect of others. He must be an example of respect for others.

A minister can help set the tone for having an organized congregation by organizing his life and work schedule during the day, primarily if he has a large part of his congregation that work different shifts. A minister must be active in his work, but a schedule that has structure that helps the congregation adhere to some structure in making appointments with him and seeing the need to plan their lives.

The minister needs to establish appointment time when he visits and when members visit him. All of this helps with making the most of every opportunity. Ephesians 5:15-16 "See then that you walk circumspectly, not as fools but as wise, redeeming the time because the days are evil."

Elders and Preachers Must Stand Together

When an eldership and preacher are as one, in fiduciary unison they stand; when these men are divided in a lack of oneness, they will surely fall, causing an immeasurable injury to the church which they have pledged to serve. Despair, which lames many Christians and congregations, results often from the lack of confidential loyalty within the leadership of elder/preacher relationships. An occasional word from the elders to the congregation, with respect to their minister's efforts and approved labor, is both essential and spiritually healthy for all concerned.

A vitally important part of a minister's mission is the necessity for sermons which exhort and rebuke members of the Lord's church. The elders must stand with the minister in his preaching of the gospel and in correctively disciplining the church in his preaching.

A minister is foolish and unstable who will allow elders to be criticized in his presence; just as elders are equally guilty and lacking in wisdom who will permit criticism of their minister without coming to the defense of one another. The often repeated adage of a wise man is appropriate for emphasis, "a dog that will bring a bone will carry a bone." The very same person who will criticize an elder to a preacher will, with the same rapidity and disrespect, criticize the preacher to an elder. The leadership of a congregation who will accept any unfavorable remarks, or discussion, of one another stands not together in the Christian spirit of oneness.

Deacons

"Deacons, likewise, are to be men worthy of respect, sincere, not indulging in much wine, and not pursuing dishonest gain.

They must keep hold of the deep truths of the faith with a clear conscience. They must first be tested; and then if there is nothing against them, let them serve as deacons. In the same way, their wives are to be women worthy of respect, not malicious talkers, but temperate and trustworthy in everything. A deacon must be the husband of but one wife and must manage his children and his household well. Those who have served well, gain an excellent standing and great assurance in their faith in Christ Jesus. "Although I hope to come to you soon, I am writing you these instructions so that, if I am delayed, you will know how people ought to conduct themselves in God's household, which is the church of the living God, the pillar and foundation of the truth." (1 Timothy 3:8-15)

Deacons Are Special Servants

The Greek noun translated "deacon" or "deacons" in our text is *diakonos*. This noun occurs twenty-nine times in the New Testament, but is only occasionally translated "deacon." The NIV translates *diakonos* as "deacon" three times in the above text (vs. 8, 10, 12) and once in Philippians (1:1). This noun in the feminine form is translated "deaconess" in Romans 16:1 in the NRSV but not in the NIV, NASB and KJV. So, how is it translated in all the other instances? Mostly by the word "servant," which is its basic meaning.

Diakonos is often used to describe one who serves at tables. This is how, for example, the servants are described at the wedding feast in Cana (John 2:5, 9). It is also used to describe those who serve God. Paul says that a brother named Tychicus was "a faithful minister *(diakonos)* and fellow servant in the Lord" (Colossians 4:7). Notice that *diakonos* is translated "minister" and not "servant" in this passage. *Diaekonos* is often used in what we might call the "servant of" passages: a servant of Christ (2 Corinthians 11:23; Colossians 4:7); a servant of God (2 Corinthians 6:4); a servant of the gospel (Ephesians 3:7; Colossians 1:23); and Paul describes himself as a servant of the church (Colossians 1:25).

In the three occurrences in 1 Timothy 3 and once in Philippians 1:1, the word seems to refer to a special servant office in the church. One thing that denotes this in 1 Timothy 3 is the qualifications of these special servants. In order to convey the idea of office or special class, our translators have traditionally transliterated the Greek word into English, which is where the English word "deacon" comes from.

All Christians should be servants of God. We can see the real meaning of service as we examine the person and work of Jesus. Jesus said, "Just as the Son of Man did not come to be served, but to serve, and to give his life as a ransom for many" (Matthew 20:28). Jesus demonstrated God's love for us when he served others (Luke 22:24-26). Some servants, however, are set apart for special ministries in the New Testament and are to be distinguished from others who serve. An example of this is the selection of the Seven by the church in Jerusalem. The apostles, who are called the Twelve by Luke, do not wish to be burdened with overseeing the benevolent needs of the widows: "So the Twelve gathered all the disciples together and said, 'It would not be right for us to neglect the ministry of the word of God in order to wait on tables. Brothers, choose seven men from among you who are known to be full of the Spirit and wisdom. We will turn this responsibility over to them and will give our attention to prayer and the ministry of the word'" (Acts 6:2-4), The verb form of the noun *diakonos* is translated "to wait" in this passage, which indicates the job of the Seven was to replace the apostles in a special servant role. The men mentioned in 1 Timothy 3:8-15 are also special servants in the church, but they do not appear to be the same as the servants in Acts 6:1-6 because their descriptions and qualifications are different. What both groups have in common is that they hold a servant office in the church.

The Qualifications of Deacons

Deacons are not the same as elders. Elders are described as overseers and shepherds of the church and deacons are not. The qualifications are slightly different as well. For example, elders are to be able to teach (I Timothy 3:2) and have believing children (Titus 1:6). The elders also represent the church in spiritual matters (Acts 20:28; I Timothy 3:5; 1 Peter 5:2), and when Paul wanted to give a vital message to the church at Ephesus (Acts 20:17), he called for the elders and not the deacons.

Since the deacons represent the church in a leadership role, they should be examples of Christian character: "Deacons, likewise, are to be men worthy of respect, sincere, not indulging in much wine, and not pursuing dishonest gain" (1 Timothy 3:8). Although Paul uses only a few descriptive terms in this verse, they cover a range of moral qualities. First, deacons are to be worthy of respect *(semnos)*, which means they are to possess the moral character and personal dignity that brings them respect. The Greek word is used to refer to the noble things a Christian is to think about (Philippians 4:8). Next, deacons are to be sincere, or "not insincere" *(me dilogous)* as it is literally in the Greek text. This is the only occurrence of this word in the Greek New Testament, which means that we do not have occurrences in other contexts of the New Testament that can help us understand the meaning here. The NIV translation of "insincere" may not give us the full meaning. The translation "double-tongued" (ASV, NASB, RSV, NRSV, KJV) is more literal but not really helpful to our understanding. Third, deacons should be men of self-control and not be addicted to such things as wine. Finally, like the elders (Titus 1:7), deacons must not pursue dishonest gain.

Deacons "must keep hold of the deep truths of the faith with a clear conscience" (1 Timothy 3:9). The translation "deep truths" in the NIV is literally "mystery" and is so translated by the RSV, NASB, ASV and KJV. What is the mystery of the faith? According to Paul's use of this word elsewhere, the mystery seems to be the new revelation of God's plan of salvation in Christ: "Now to him who is able to establish you by my gospel and the proclamation of Jesus Christ, according to the revelation of the mystery hidden for long ages past" (Romans 16:25). Furthermore, Paul says that

God "made known to us the mystery of his will according to his good pleasure, which he purposed in Christ" (Ephesians 1:9). This mystery is not something that is mysterious, but something that was once hidden and is now made known by revelation. The gospel has been revealed through the inspired apostles and prophets and the content of their message is contained in the documents of the New Testament. It is the faith that has once for all been delivered to the saints (Jude 3).

Paul says that deacons must be tested: "They must first be tested; and then if there is nothing against them, let them serve as deacons" (1 Timothy 3:10). What is the testing in this verse? This probably refers to the examination and approval by the congregation. The verb translated "test" *(dokimazo)* has the sense of examination in many occurrences in the New Testament. This is evident in the following occurrences (the English translation of the verb is in italics): "Then, when I arrive, I will give letters of introduction to the men you *approve* and send them with your gift to Jerusalem" (1 Corinthians 16:3); *"Test* everything. Hold on to the good" (1 Thessalonians 5:21); "A man ought to *examine* himself before he eats of the bread and drinks of the cup" (1 Corinthians 11:28).

There is some question about whether Paul also gives qualifications for the deacons' wives. Are the women of verse 11 the wives of the deacons as the NIV and KJV translate it? Or, does it refer to the women of the church as the NASB and NRSV translate it? In New Testament Greek, a man refers to his wife as his woman and a woman refers to her husband as her man. The Greek word can mean either woman or wife and sometimes it is difficult to know which one. Some believe the word does not refer to either women in general or wives of the deacons, but to women deacons instead. For example, a woman named Phoebe is called a servant of the church in Romans 16:1, and some believe, like the translators of the NRSV, that this is an example of women deacons. As we have already noted, the word *diakonos* does not normally refer to an office in the church and is not even used with reference to the women in 1 Timothy 3:11. The context must determine whether the author is referring to a special class of servants. This does not seem to be the case here because Paul continues with his discussion of the male deacons in the next verse, which lends support to the idea that he is referring to the wives of the deacons.

The Example of Leadership

Deacons are leaders and they are mentioned when Paul addresses the Philippian church (Philippians 1:1). Those who hold an office of service in the church have a special responsibility to set an example for the whole church. This means that if someone serves in leadership he must be willing to make the necessary commitment that leadership demands. Leaders who fail in their example have a very negative impact on the rest of the church and the community. Perhaps this is why Peter commanded elders to be examples (1 Peter 5:3). It has been my experience that churches often allow men to serve as deacons who do not measure up to the same standard of faithfulness that is required of other leaders. Because these men are not elders or preachers, some make the false assumption that deacons are not required to meet a very high standard of commitment and faithfulness.

There are areas of concern that churches should have relative to a deacon's leadership example. The preacher/elders should preach on these topics before deacons are ever selected. The purpose of mentioning these areas of concern is to encourage the nomination of men who will provide a good example of commitment to the church. If a deacon's faith and practice is not what it should be, then the church is sending the wrong signal by appointing such a man to a position of leadership.

Conclusion

In regard to leadership in the church of Christ, has something been lost along the way? I believe it has; we must return to the desire to please the Lord. All of us may be pressured from time to time to please ourselves. We sometimes focus too much on our future than on our goal to serve the Lord. I may get caught up in how can I, as minister, keep my job and stay with this congregation in order that I can retire here or build a kingdom unto myself. I may, as an elder, be motivated by power and self-worth to the degree of feeling that a minister is gaining too much influence and power which may threaten my position of authority. We must both remember that the church belongs to Christ and He delegates areas of responsibility to us. It is not our church. May we work together in maintaining that the organizational structure of the church of Christ can still be a means of identifying the church as God's one body.

Luis R. Lugo

Luis R. Lugo was born October 25, 1946 in Charllet Amalie, St. Thomas, United States Virgin Islands. He's been married to Andrea C. Lugo for over 46 years. They have five beautiful children Tito, Kyle Stephen (deceased), Robin, Michael Wellington, and Mark Antonio, and 3 grandchildren, Ashley, Asia and Fendi.

His academic credentials include Thomas Alva Edison High School in Philadelphia, PA 1965. He attended Sunset School of Religious Study, Lubbock, TX, 1968-1970, International Seminary, Orlando, FL, 1981 Trinity Seminary, Indiana, 1983, Southern, 1984, Kansas City Community College 1994, and American Theological Seminary, 2003. He has both a master and doctorate in theology. He is a much sought out speaker for workshops, lectureships and Gospel Meetings.

He has been preaching the Gospel for forty-two years and his experiences are numerous. He served at St. Croix Church of Christ 1971-1976, Alton Park Church of Christ, Chattanooga, TN, 1976-1979, West Adair Church of Christ, Valdosta, GA, 1980-1981, Highland Avenue Church of Christ, Tampa, FL, 1981-1989 Roswell Avenue Church of Christ, Kansas City, KS, 1991-1997, Monroe Street Church of Christ, Chicago, IL 1997-2008 and now presently at Bell Fork Church of Christ, Jacksonville, NC.

His favorite hobby is fishing and reading. His published works are:

The Five-fold Work of the Evangelist
The Five-fold Work of the Elder
The Blessed Life

CHAPTER 9

The Forgotten Commandment

Luis R. Lugo

—⚊—

Introduction

Everything in this world has a purpose! By purpose, I am speaking of an objective, aim, goal and reason. Without this, one would never know the significance for the existence, necessity or the objective for why it is in existence. Thus, in order for something to be conducive or germane to why it was produced, made or manufactured, one must not only know why it exists, but how is it implemented to accomplish the very purpose for which it has been created or made.

Thus, we must have a working knowledge of the intent of its progenitor. So, if the church is to understand its divine purpose, there must be some instruction manual, some plan of operation by which those who are to benefit can know, if and when they have received the benefit, to make sure it is operating according to the inventors purpose and how to correct it when it goes against the intent.

When we speak of the mission of the church, we are speaking not of its purpose, which is to glorify God (Ephesians 3:20-21), but how it glorifies God. In other words, how DOES the church, both in its universal aspect as well as in its local entity, GLORIFY God?

We need to make sure we understand first what the church is, then what is the ultimate purpose and how it makes that purpose applicable to the church today?

When Jesus came into the coast of Cesarean of Philippi as recorded by the tax gather Matthew, Jesus demanded of His disciples what people thought of Him? In their response to Him about the people's perception, they said, "some say you are John the Baptist, some say Elijah, Jeremiah or one of the prophets"! Now notice several things about where the question was asked, then the response. Caesarea was the name that was given to this section of the country by Herod when it was ceded to him. Later, Philip did some work and it became known as Cesaria Philippi, the birth place of Pan, Bal and one of the great centers for emperor worship. In the midst of Idolatry, pagan culture and emperor worship, Jesus challenges the people's knowledge of who He is. The disciples responded by giving the misconception that Jesus was not the Messiah, but that He was just a messenger or the fore runner of the messiah. They viewed Jesus with a skewed concept, to which Jesus wants to know, what is your view? What do you say? It was here that Peter recognizes that Jesus was the Son of God and so he confesses Jesus as the Son of God, to which Jesus responds and pronounces a blessing, "flesh and blood did not reveal this unto thee but my Father which is in heaven"! The question is how did God reveal this to you, Simon? Certainly, it could have been done in a variety of ways, but we must conclude that Peter just naturally observed the miracles that Jesus did, the things and ways He taught, and His impact on the life of the community. There are several component parts to this prophecy:

What did Jesus mean by "church"? What did those who heard Him understand by that term that Jesus used? What then is the church?

The term "ekklesia" was a familiar term used to designate an assembly, a body, a congregation, a society, and in some cases a family or tribe. To the Greeks, this term carried with it the idea of an assembly, a society where the members were composed of those individuals who were free. The free may have gotten their freedom as a gift from their masters, or they may have purchased it. Only those who were free could participate in the decision making of the society. Thus, when there was a decision to be made, the town crier would summon those who were free to come and participate in the decision making process. Thus, those who understood the Greek concept would know that Jesus was talking about making a society of free individuals. The question is, free from what? The believer is set free from the eternal consequences of eternal damnation (John 8:31-32).

To the Hebrew audience, they understood the Greek equivalent meant a congregation under a sovereign. In this situation, God is the Authority and Israel was the congregation. The third way to understand this term is in its English comprehension. The English translation for church is not an actual translation from the term ekklesia, but from the German derivative "Kurios" where the k sound was dropped and turned into the c sound "che." The term Kurios means, "by strong one, lord, and messiah." The church then could be translated; the assembly of the free under the authority of God, invested with the strength of the Lord. Thus, the church is not a weak entity, but composed of free, authoritative, powerful people given the task of conquering the world for Jesus with His Gospel (Matt. 28:18-20; Luke 24:44-47; Mk. 16:15-16; John 20:21; Acts 1:8).

Why then is it that the missionary work of the church is so anemic and in the majority of congregations, non-existent? Why do we spend more money on brick and motor than we do about mission work? Why are there nations who have never heard the name Jesus? Why are there 500 million Chinese who are more familiar with Coke, but not the Real Thing, Jesus? Can there be a correlation between the anemic churches growth among us that die, due to the fact of our anemic concept of mission work? Why it is that less than one cent of every dollar given in contributions is used to take the Gospel to every creature? Why is it that the early church grew at the pace it did in the first century with less resources, including man power, less means of communicating and transportation, as well as outreach resources such as televisions, radios, internet, etc., and yet after some twenty-three years, Paul the apostle could boast that the whole world had heard the Gospel! (Col. 1:23)

We need leaders who will restore the mandate of Jesus to carry the Gospel to the world, not just to the American continent. Leaders in the church must come to grips with the fact that in America, less than 10% of the world's <u>population resides while 90% resides out in the rest of the world</u> and yet we have 10% of all Gospel preachers trying to preach to 90% of the world's population, while 90% of Gospel preachers are preaching to 10% of the world's population.

Why it is that it takes 14 Jehovah's witness, 27 Baptist, 4 Seven Day Adventist, 2 Mormons to support one missionary, while it takes 127,000 members of the church to support one missionary in the world?

Why is it that denominational churches have thousands of missionaries, schools, hospitals, radio, and television programs in the world and we have less than 300 missionaries? By the same token, we have a handful of radio and television programs and only a few schools and no hospitals that I am aware of?

Why are we so consumed with buildings and facilities while missionaries have to travel up and down the highways of this country begging churches to equip them to take the Gospel to the world, instead of churches looking to send men and women to the world equipped to handle the task?

Why do we accept the concept that someone has the right to hear the Gospel twice before someone hears it once?

Beloved, the church has failed because of its materialistic concept more than for any other reason. We have the financial resources; we have spent over 20 billion on brick and mortar. We can support two or more full-time preaches, elders, janitors, secretaries, accountants, even lawyers, but cannot support not even a part-time one. How can we profess love of God, Christ and sinners while every 7 seconds, people are dying without Christ?

Where should the priority of the church and church leaders lay? Why do we have all kinds of lectureships, conferences, workshop on everything that affects people, but when did you attend a workshop, conference or lectureship on the subject of mission work? How many leaders have a projected plan to take the Gospel to the world? How many are planning to take the Gospel to a town, city or nation? How many people are being prepared or trained to be missionaries? How many preparations on financial matters are in progress?

How many areas have been targeted by local leaders to take the Gospel, and have selected a person, family or group who have dedicated themselves to going and providing the resources for their welfare?

How many leaders have prepared their congregations for supporting and being involved in the process of world missions?

The daunting task of too many leaders is self-preservation of their local work and has forgotten the Lord's emphasis on world mission! What will it take to get the church of today to be ready unto every good work? When will leaders discover that the reason the church was the fastest growing group in America, right after

WWII, was due to the missionary effort of those military men who came home recognizing the need to take the Gospel to the world they have just left?

In the words of the song, "Open Mine Eyes That I Might See," the leaders of today must open their eyes to the more than 25 million people in the Caribbean who need the Gospel as well as the rest of the billions the world over?

John Davis Marshall

John Davis Marshall is the grandson of a former slave. He was born and raised in Medon, Tennessee. He is married to the former Priscilla Jackson of Blytheville, Arkansas. They have four children (Terrence, Marrkus, Jondreia and Johnathan) and nine grandchildren.

MINISTRY

John is the CEO of the **Solomon Society**, a 501c3 Non-profit Corporation, developed to educate and nurture individuals into the practical relevancy of the wisdom of God. Solomon Society provides life coaching through teaching, training, workshops, forums, seminars, support groups, and social media.

John is an author, counselor, editor, life coach, minister, and relationship consultant. With more than 5,000 presentations, he has inspired audiences in 1 foreign country, twenty-six states, and 156 cities. Weekly, he hosts two Internet radio programs: "Grace Nurture" and Verse-by-Verse." He has successfully served churches in Alabama, Arkansas, Georgia, North Carolina, South Carolina, and Tennessee.

EDUCATION

John studied at Freed-Hardeman University (BS), Theological University of America (MA), University of Memphis, and Southern Christian University. His research paper, *"Single-mothering Stimulates A Positive Family Networking Within Black Families"* was selected and presented at the Annual Graduate Research Symposium at Memphis State University.

WRITINGS

He has authored and published *twelve* books:

"Good and Angry" - *A personal guide to anger management*

"The Power of the Tongue" – *What you say is what you get*

"God, Listen" – *Prayers that God always answers*
[includes a 50-day addiction recovery guide]

"Final Answer"

"Success is a God Idea"

"Show Me the Money" – *7 exercises that build economic strength.*

"God Knows" – *There is no need to worry.*

"My God" – *Who He is will change your life.*

"Faith, Family, & Finances" Vol. One – *Essential truths that lead to passionate happiness.*

"Faith, Family, & Finances" Vol. Two - *The mess we are in and how to get out of it!*

"A Queen In Search of A King" –
Go ahead and ask Him for a date!

"Church Matters" – *Passionate Pleadings That Prepare Us For The Future*

John is the author of **BLUEPRINTS**—*Building the Kingdom Lifestyle,* a Bible school curriculum for ages sixteen to adults. He serves as editor for the **Solomon Society** monthly newsletter, staff writer for the **Revivalist Magazine,** and on the Alumni Advisory Board of Freed-Hardeman University.

CHAPTER 10

Now, What?
After We Discussed,
We Still Disagreed!

John Davis Marshall

—⁓—

What would you think if you saw the following? There will be a public discussion examining the following question: *How must I treat my brother with whom I have a sincere disagreement?*

Brother Truth N. Error, Sr. advocates –

Unity, as taught within New Testament scripture, requires a Christian to cease to worship/fellowship with one who hosts an opposing belief. Christians can worship/fellowship only with others when they agree on doctrinal issues. Therefore, Christians who do not believe that worshippers can, with God's approval, clap their hands and use multiple microphones while singing must discontinue worshiping together with others who believe that worshippers can, with God's approval, clap their hands and use multiple microphones while singing.

Brother Truth N. Error, Jr. advocates -

Unity, as taught within New Testament scripture, authorizes a Christian to worship/fellowship with one who hosts an opposing belief. Christians can worship/fellowship with others, even when they disagree on doctrinal issues. Therefore, Christians who do not believe that worshippers can, with God's approval, clap their hands and use multiple microphones while singing may continue to worship together with others who believe that worshippers can, with God's approval, clap their hands and use multiple microphones while singing.

How must I treat my brother with whom I have a sincere disagreement?

How long has it been since you read, studied, and learned a truth from scripture? Whatever that truth was, before you learned that truth, you did not know that truth. If someone had engaged you in a discussion of that truth, before you learned that truth, what would you have said? Likely, you would have denied that truth. Definitely, you could not have provided an objective understanding. Certainly, you would not have been able to take the position on that truth that you now take. How should people have treated you before you learned that truth? How should people treat you now, before you learn other truths that you will soon learn? Should they have labeled you as a false teacher? Should they have refused fellowship with you because you did not (for you could not have) believe as they believed?

All truths are not readily discernible. Knowledge of some truths requires practice and exercise (Hebrews 5:13-14). Prior to sufficient practice and exercise, those truths lie outside of the believer's conscious and conscience awareness.

The apostle Peter declared that some truths are hard to understand (2 Peter 3:14-16). Prior to being taught and becoming stable, understanding lies outside of the believer's conscious and conscience awareness. Proper understanding comes only after study. Even the apostle Peter himself did not immediately understand what God was trying to get him to understand (Acts 10:9-21). Though Peter preached oneness, he did not understand it (Acts 2:17, 21, 39). And it seems that after he understood it, he required time before he came to practice it (Galatians 2:11-14). How should we treat honest brothers and sister while they are coming into their knowledge of certain Biblical truths?

Well-intentioned, spiritually-minded students of scripture often disagree as to the teaching of a particular passage. Seasoned scholars will continue to disagree. In the meantime, how should they treat each other?

Some subscribe to this position. They wholeheartedly believe that unity, as taught within New Testament scripture, authorizes a Christian to worship/fellowship with one who hosts an opposing belief. Therefore, they argue that Christians can continue to worship/fellowship with others even when they disagree on doctrinal issue. Thus, Christians may continue to worship/fellowship together with those who believe differently.

To the same questions, others think differently. They subscribe to this position. These wholeheartedly believe that unity, as taught within New Testament scripture, requires a Christian to cease to worship/fellowship with one who hosts an opposing belief. Christians can continue to worship/fellowship only with others when they agree on doctrinal issues. Thus, Christians must discontinue worship/fellowship together with those who believe differently.

Human understanding is fragile. Disagreement is a constant. Misunderstanding is a given. Conflict will continually surface. Therefore, opposition is inherent in the church arena.

Conflict naturally surfaces when one person learns something new about another person. For example, when a wife learns that her husband wants to buy a new truck while she, by the same token, wants to purchase a new living room suite, conflict erupts. When one believer discovers that another believer has different beliefs, conflict surfaces.

Optional Issues

Leaders will always experience differences and opposition from followers over "leader-follower" issues. "Leader-follower" issues are non-biblically prescribed optional issues. These issues may be sensitive, but are not salvation issues. How should I respond?

The apostle Paul and Barnabas dealt with a leader-follower issue. Paul invited Barnabas to go, inspect, and give spiritual aid to the believers to whom they had earlier ministered (Acts 15:36). Barnabas thought John Mark should go with them (Acts 15:37). Paul disagreed vehemently (Acts 15:38a).

Taking John Mark with them was a "leader-follower" issue. It was just a personal matter of policy and procedure. Two godly believers disagreed over a "leader-follower" issue. Consider these guiding principles.

If you are one who most often responds with your head from your perception of the need, keep advancing the kingdom work. Very likely, Paul most often responded with his head from his perception of the need. Previously, Paul had been the rejected one (Acts 15:38b, 13:4-13). On this later occasion, John Mark had abandoned him. Likely, now Paul thought they needed one who had proven to be more dependable than John Mark.

Paul disagreed, but he kept advancing the kingdom work. He took Silas and traveled the land route (Acts 15:40-41). In spite of his differing over a leader-follower issue, Paul kept advancing the kingdom work (Acts 15:41b).

If you are one who most often responds with your heart from your passion of nature, keep advancing the kingdom work. Very likely, Barnabas most often responded with his heart from his passion of nature. Previously, Barnabas had vouched for a rejected one (Acts 9:22-27; Acts 4:36). On this earlier occasion, he had reached out and validated the ministry of Paul. Likely, now Barnabas thought that they should nurture John back into ministry.

Barnabas disagreed, but he kept advancing the kingdom work. He took Mark and traveled the water route (Acts 15:39). In spite of his differing over a leader-follower issue, Barnabas kept advancing the kingdom work (1 Corinthians 9:6), Galatians 2:1, Colossians 4:10).

Personal preferences must remain secondary to the advancing of the kingdom work. Always seek the blessings of the church for your ventures (Acts 15:40b-41). Never allow a personal disagreement to become an obstacle to nurturing other believers. Years later, it was obvious that the estrangement between Paul and John Mark remained no more (2 Timothy 4:11). He had adequately redeemed himself.

Let's consider how not to respond. Never respond in a manner that mistreats God. Miriam differed with Moses (Numbers 20:1-10). Unfortunately, Moses responded in a way that violated God (Psalms 106:33). Though Miriam initiated the conflict, but because of Moses' misbehavior, God denied him entrance into the Promised Land.

Never respond in a manner that mistreats people. The apostles disagreed with how the Samaritans treated Jesus (Luke 9:51-56). James and John wanted to call down fire from heaven and consume them. Jesus rebuked them for that thought. For, He had come to save lives, not destroy lives. Though the Samaritans initiated the conflict, but because of their misbehavior, Jesus rebuked His disciples.

When people differ and oppose because of lack of information, then teach them (Matthew 22:23-33). The Sadducees were ignorant of the passages of scripture and the power of God.

When people differ and oppose because of lack of integrity, then confront them (Matthew 21:23-27). The chief priests and elders of the people were insincere.

Obligatory Issues

It would be nice if all disagreements were over non-biblically prescribed optional issues. Unfortunately, all differences are not about "leader-follower" issues. Some issues are over biblically prescribed obligated issues. These are sensitive issues and salvation issues.

Some men came down from Jerusalem of Judea to Antioch of Syria and taught that God required the Gentiles to be circumcised and obey the Law of Moses in order to be saved (Acts 15:1). Paul and Barnabas sternly disagreed (Acts 15:2a). While in Antioch, they debated the issue, but did not reach a unanimous conclusion. Therefore, they deemed it necessary to travel some 333 miles to go up to Jerusalem to further discuss this issue with the apostles and elders.

Circumcision according to the Law of Moses was being taught as a "biblically prescribed obligated issue." It was not just a matter of personal preference, it was a theological issue. Two groups of believers disagreed over whether this was a "biblically prescribed obligated" issue.

Occasionally, believers will disagree over whether a teaching is indeed a "biblically prescribed obligated issue." We must objectively discuss our differences when biblically prescribed obligated issues are involved. Biblically prescribed obligated issues are not just sensitive issues, but they are salvation issues. How do we objectively discuss?

We must discuss our differences in view of the authoritative action of God. God chose the Gentiles to hear and believe (Acts 15:7). He gave them the Holy Spirit to signify His choice (Acts 15:8, Acts 10:44-48). Also, God cleansed their hearts by faith (Acts 15:9). In this instance, the paramount question always is, "What has God done?"

Religious teachings are false when they contradict the actions of God. Requiring the Gentiles to become circumcised and obey the Law of Moses contradicted what God had done. God had accepted the Gentiles granting them repentance just as He had the Jews. His giving of the Holy Spirit testified that He had accepted them just as He had accepted the Jews. Also, God had cleansed the hearts of the Gentiles by faith just as He had the Jews.

We must discuss our differences in view of the authoritative advice of the apostles and prophets, the spokesmen of God. They advised nurturing the Gentiles in the faith according to the word of God (Acts 15:19, 13-17). Also, they advised nurturing the Gentiles in the faith according to the wisdom of God (Acts 15:19, 18). In this instance, the paramount question always is, "What has God said through the advice of the apostles?"

Religious teachings are false when they contradict the advice of the apostles. Requiring the Gentiles to be circumcised and obey the Law of Moses would have contradicted what the apostles advised. The apostles advised against placing a yoke of the Law of Moses upon the Gentiles that the Jews were unable to bear. God had released the Jews from the burden of the Law of Moses. The apostles advised that the Gentiles should be accepted on the basis of their having turned to God just as the Jews had.

God expects each Christian to resist false religious teachings. Why should we resist false religious teachings?

False teachings will disturb the soul of believers (Acts 15:24). The word "disturb" translated literally meant to agitate, terrify

145

or vex. It meant to trouble with various emotions such as fear (Luke 1:12; 24:38; Acts 17:8; Galatians 1:7). What results from a disturbed soul?

A disturbed soul will lead believers to deny the sufficiency of their present relationship. In their situation, it was a sufficient relationship that was based upon grace and faith (Acts 15:8-11). Also, a disturbed soul will lead believers to deny the insufficiency of their past relationship. In their situation, it was an insufficient relationship based upon circumcision and the keeping of the Law of Moses (Acts 3:22; Galatians 5:1-4).

Certainly, false teachings disturb the soul of believers; but more than that, false teachings will unsettle the soul of believers. "Unsettling" was translated from a compound word that meant (1) back and (2) prepare. It meant to prepare to go back. It literally meant, (1) to move and carry off all goods and furniture of the home as if to quit the residence (2) to pack up baggage as to return to a previous residence (3) to reverse allegiance. What results from an unsettled soul?

Unsettled souls lead believers to depart from their present relationship. They departed from a sufficient relationship that was based upon grace and faith. In other words, they quit trusting in Jesus for their salvation (Galatians 5:1-4). Also, unsettled souls lead believers to depart to their past relationship. They departed to an insufficient relationship that was based upon circumcision and law keeping. In other words, they returned to trusting in Moses for salvation.

When believers disagree over "biblically prescribed obligated issues," they must maintain their spiritual integrity.

Our attitude indicates our spiritual integrity; therefore, we must maintain our spiritual relationship attitude. The Holy Spirit inspired the apostles to call others, even those who were teaching error, their brethren (Acts 15:7; 13). They were teaching falsely, but they were not called false teachers. The apostles did not call them hyphenated (erring brethren, nor false teachers) brethren.

Our action indicates our spiritual integrity; therefore, we must maintain our spiritual relationship action. The Holy Spirit moved them to receive each other and discuss until they agreed (Acts 15:4, 22). They continued to fellowship throughout their study of the word.

Our relationship continues long after we end fellowship. To what extent can I fellowship with others and not endorse all of their beliefs and behaviors? Tolerance is an attribute of God (Romans 2:4, Ephesians 4:2; 2 Peter 3:9). God wants you to willingly discuss differences in brotherly love. Discuss until you die.

What is our charge? Believers have a divine mandate to advance truth (1 Thessalonians 5:21, 2 Timothy 4:1-5; Jude 3). Also, believers have a divine mandate to oppose error (Ephesians 6:11, Titus 1:7-11; 2 John 9-11).

We must objectively discuss our differences when biblically prescribed obligated issues are involved. We must discover the differences. We can debate the difference. We do this in an effort to decide about the differences. God wants you to discuss until an acceptable conclusion is reached. When we are unable to conclude, we must discuss until we die.

I am not suggesting that we should discuss until we die from the fatigue of the discussion. Neither am I suggesting that we should discuss our differences every time we communicate. But, I would suggest that with some degree of frequency, we ought to discuss our difference.

Several years ago, the brethren in a particular state came together to discuss marriage, divorce, and (re) marriage. I informed one of the disputants that they would accomplish more if they would: (1) first discuss how they should treat a brother with whom they had an honest disagreement and (2) agree to once a year come together and discuss marriage, divorce, and (re) marriage. But in the meantime, they should decide not to divide over their difference. I did not convince him. Since I did not reside in that state and was not a part of the discussion, I did not convince the other preachers either. I should not even have to tell you what resulted. Nothing! They ran into the meeting but stumbled out along the same fault lines they have always lived by.

Solving disagreements may always be as simple as the disagreement in Antioch. Solving them may not always be this satisfactory. Solving some disagreements may never be forth coming. Nevertheless, we must keep discussing in view of the actions of God and the advice of the apostles. When we allow the example of Jesus to provide clarity and interpret the actions of God and the advice of the apostles, amazingly many textual misunderstandings are solved.

Let's review. We have learned that believers occasionally disagree over "non-biblically prescribed optional" (sensitive) issues. Before you begin to discuss, decide how you will continually advance the kingdom work.

Also, we have learned that they sometime disagree over "biblically prescribed obligated issues." Objectively discuss the differences. These issues are not just sensitive, but are salvation issues.

With whom did you recently discuss differences of "non-biblically prescribed optional issues?" With whom did you recently discuss differences of "biblically prescribed obligated issues?" What was the issue and how did the discussion proceed?

What About Withdrawing Fellowship?

When and from whom do we withdraw fellowship? We must withdraw fellowship from those who are intentionally immoral (1 Corinthians 5:1-13). And, we must withdraw fellowship from those who are intentionally negligent (2 Thessalonians 3:6-15). Also, we must withdraw fellowship from those who are intentionally divisive (Titus 3:8-11).

Cleavon Matthews

Cleavon Matthews is married to the former Christy Stephens-McVey. Their blended family includes four daughters, two sons, and one granddaughter. Cleavon has been preaching the Gospel since 1992. He currently serves as minster to the Northwest Church of Christ in Trotwood, Ohio. He has been privileged to serve churches in Tennessee, Mississippi, Florida, and Ohio.

Dr. Matthews is an advocate for education. He obtained a diploma in Nursing from Baptist School of Nursing in 1994 and is a Registered Nurse. Brother Matthews completed his Bachelor of Science in Bible from Crichton College. He has also completed two masters' degrees from Amridge University in ministry and leadership. Brother Matthews earned a Doctor of Ministry Degree from Amridge in 2009. His dissertation is entitled: "Reaffirming the Biblical Role of Men and Women in Family, Church, and Society."

Dr. Matthews' ministry focus is in the areas of leadership development, evangelism, mentoring, writing, and preaching. It is his dream to establish and create a counseling center directed at serving individuals, families, and organizations with a variety of emotional, relational, and practical challenges.

CHAPTER 11

Men and Women in the
New Testament Family and Church

Cleavon Matthews

—⁓—

The New Testament implores the language of family to describe the church. Vern Sheridan Poythress, Professor of New Testament Interpretation at Westminster Theological Seminary, points readers toward several New Testament texts demonstrating this analogy: God is Father (Matthew 6:9), the redeemed are children of God (Galatians 4:1-7), saints have an intimate family fellowship with God (Romans 8:14-17), saints have the privilege of reflecting the Father's holy character (1 Peter 1:14-17), and only Christians can cry "Abba, Father" (Romans 8:15).[1]

---

[1] Vern Sheridan Poythress, "The Church as Family: Why Male Leadership in the Family Requires Male Leadership in the Church," in *Recovering Biblical Manhood and Womanhood*, ed. John Piper and Wayne Grudem (Wheaton, IL: Crossway Books, 1991), 233-234.

There is a close relationship between the organizational design of the family and the church. Everett Ferguson writes:

> The church in its organization reflects God's plan for the family. In fact, the church is described as a family. The Greek word "<u>oikos</u>" may refer to a house, a dwelling place, a building; and in this sense on occasion refers to the dwelling place, a building; and on some occasion refers to the dwelling place of deity, a temple. The word also may refer to those who dwell in a house, the household or family.[2]

Vern Sheridan Poythress agrees with Ferguson. He is convinced that in 1 Timothy the reference is to those in the church family. He writes:

> But in the context of 1 Timothy, the idea of household order and arrangements is obviously the most prominent. The order of the church is analogous to the order of a human household. Members of the church are to treat one another as they would members of their own family (1 Timothy 5:1-2). They are to care for one another in need (1 Timothy 5:5, 16). The overseers are to be men skillful at managing the household of God, as demonstrated by their earlier skill with their own immediate families (1 Timothy 3:1-7).[3]

In fact, a failure to acknowledge the similarities and connections shared by the family and the church has contributed to the confusion between the role of men and women. Alexander Strauch describes the scenario when he writes:

> Many people don't understand the New Testament's view of men and women in the church because they don't understand the intimate relationship between the individual

---

[2] Everett Ferguson, *Women in the Church*, 56.
[3] Vern Sheridan Poythress, "The Church as Family," 235-236.

family and the extended family, which is the local church. Just as Paul teaches masculine leadership in the individual family, he teaches masculine leadership in the extended local church family. So an understanding of leadership in the family is essential to an understanding of leadership in the church family.[4]

It is important to increase the understanding of this relationship among the men and women actively involved in the Church of Christ.

An important understanding is the model of male leadership in both the family and the church. Everett Ferguson describes this idea:

Leadership in the church corresponds to leadership in the family. As indicated above, the leadership in the family derives from the pattern set by Christ and the Church. Since the church is a family, we should expect the same principles of organization to be operative in the church as apply to the family, and indeed this is true. Leadership in the church is given to male family heads, not to all males.[5]

Therefore, a deficiency in family leadership such as single parent homes, divorce, spiritually mixed marriages, and abandonment of responsibility will adversely affect the church. Alexander Strauch explains:

It is becoming increasingly difficult to find biblically qualified and prepared men to assume the responsibilities of church eldership and deaconship. The hyper-busyness of our culture holds many of our men in a spiritual death grip: "The cult of busyness and activism that infects Christians so much today is one of the greatest barriers to the church

---

[4] Alexander Strauch, *Men and Women: Equal Yet Different*, 71.
[5] Everett Ferguson, *Women in the Church*, 59.

becoming what it should be. Too many men have no time for Bible reading, prayer, or church family leadership. Some don't even have time for their families. When men neglect their community leadership responsibilities within the church community, a tragic loss and a stunning victory for the evil one occurs.[6]

Evangelists

Evangelists are included in God's family.[7] Paul refers to Timothy, an evangelist, as 'his son in the faith.'[8] Timothy is also included in the house or household of God.[9] Evangelists serve God's people within the family.[10] Harold R. Redd, an African-American evangelist among Churches of Christ, cautions Christian ministers to remember their charge as God's servants to serve and sacrifice for His people.[11]

Evangelists are leaders in the local church. However, debate surrounds the role of the evangelist within Churches of Christ. Everett Ferguson excludes the evangelist from a leadership role within the church.[12] Harold R. Redd explains the history of the debate:

White churches generally believed the elders of the church exercised primary authority in the churches. African-American churches were generally led by the parson or the evangelist. J. S. Winston, at the fiftieth Annual National Lectureship of African-American Churches

---

[6] Alexander Strauch, *Men and Women: Equal Yet Different*, 75.

[7] In Churches of Christ, evangelists are also known as preachers and ministers.

[8] 1 Timothy 1:2.

[9] 1 Timothy 3:15.

[10] 1 Timothy 5:1-2.

[11] Harold R. Redd, "Leadership Training For Congregational Transition: A Case Study in An African-American Church" (D. Min. thesis, Abilene Christian University, 2000), 53.

[12] Ferguson assigns exclusive leadership to the elders. Everett Ferguson, *Women in the Church*, 60.

of Christ, talked about the history of that leadership issue. In summary, he explained how white elders often ordained elders in African-American churches to help oversee or watch the preacher, who was in many cases the preacher for the black church and the custodian for the white church. These elder ordinations and the whole approach to appointing elders was strongly resented by African-American ministers in the Churches of Christ. Many preached sermons against elders' rights to ordain elders and about the biblical authority of the evangelist because of this issue. When elders in African-American churches perceived themselves as having authority over the evangelist, power struggles resulted, and many black preachers became hesitant to ordain elders. Fortunately, this hesitancy is changing as more African-American ministers learn that one gains power by losing it and are more willing to risk control for the development that results when people are trained and empowered.[13]

The evangelist often serves as the primary leader. Redd writes:

Many African-American Churches of Christ, even ones with elders and deacons, have functioned with a man at the top. This arrangement would not have presented a problem for African culture, but has conflicted with European-American concepts of leadership.[14]

Regardless to one's view, God ordained the role of evangelists,[15] the evangelist, especially in African-American churches, has played a crucial role,[16] and the evangelist has a role outside of the pulpit.[17] In this writers own experience as an evangelist,

---

[13] Harold R. Redd, "Leadership Training," 14-15.
[14] Ibid, 54.
[15] Ibid, 50.
[16] Ibid, 51.
[17] Ibid, 52.

the congregation often looks to him for vision and guidance concerning the direction of the church.[18]

The work of the evangelist attests to his leadership role. God gave the church evangelists in order to prepare the members to do spiritual work.[19] Luis R. Lugo, an African-American evangelist in the Churches of Christ, places the work of the evangelist in five categories based on the New Testament Epistles of 1 and 2 Timothy and Titus:

1. Proclaimer—that is, he is to preach, herald, proclaim the gospel

2. Trainer—He is to train the local church

3. Organizer—He is to "set in order the things that are lacking"

4. Defender—He is to be set for the defense of the Gospel

5. Discipliner——He is to discipline heretics[20]

Evangelists and elders work together. The evangelist and elders are working together in the ministry context of most thriving Churches of Christ. They have a shared vision and set of values to help guide them toward their goals and objectives. Luis R. Lugo attests to the importance of the relationship between the evangelist and elders when he writes:

> Once elders are ordained, the congregation must realize that elders are not superior to the evangelist. It is precisely here that the evangelist and elders must have a strong working relationship, for there are many weak people in the body, who because of likes and dislikes, will pit the

---

[18] Ibid, 52.

[19] Ephesians 4:11-12.

[20] Luis R. Lugo, *The Five Fold Work of the Evangelist: God's Church Administration* (Homewood, IL: L&L Publication, 1999), 16-17.

evangelist against the elders and vice versa. If the relationship is not right the church will suffer...He does not
relinquish his authority because elders have been ordained!
Elders die, disqualify themselves, move, get old and lose
interest. Therefore, the training and development of men
to serve as elders is an ongoing process.[21]

Clearly, a relationship of trust based on mutual love, care,
accountability, and respect is vital to sustaining this important
Christian relationship.[22]

Evangelists are men and not women. However, Robert M.
Randolph, a member of the Churches of Christ, would like to hear
the voices of women in our pulpits.[23] Julia Craig-Horne listed a
number of arguments both for and against women clergy.[24] Since the
evangelist is a leader within God's family with the aforementioned
responsibilities, this excludes women from assuming this role. The
principles of male headship are applicable in this area as well.[25]

Elders

The New Testament uses various terms to describe elders[26]
such as overseers[27], shepherds[28], pastors[29], and bishops[30]. There are

---

[21] Ibid, 89.

[22] Ibid, 88. Lugo describes this as a close intimate relationship.

[23] Robert M. Randolph, "Why Women Should Be Preaching in Churches of
Christ," 205.

[24] Julia Craig-Horne, "Pew to the Pulpit," 12-31.

[25] Ibid, 27. Craig-Horne states, "The scriptures provide clear and concise principles of headship in the church, home, and community," when arguing against
women clergy.

[26] James 5:14.

[27] 1 Peter 5:2.

[28] 1 Peter 5:2.

[29] Ephesians 4:11.

[30] Philippians 1:1. The NIV uses overseers; however, the KJV and NKJV uses
Bishops.

several dissertations addressing the role of elders within Churches of Christ,[31] however, none of them address the role of men and women.

Elders are men and not women. Alexander Strauch correctly asserts that a Biblical eldership is exclusively male.[32] However, in many denominations women have been ordained in this office.[33] There are significant indications from the New Testament that only men meet the requirements for this important office. One of the qualifications for being an elder is being 'the husband of one wife.'[34] Furthermore, elders must demonstrate their ability to lead their families.[35] Luis R. Lugo makes this important observation when he writes:

> Within the home, the man who would be an elder receives on the job training in anticipation of becoming an elder in the house of the Lord. Let us never forget that the church is the Lord's house and that the men who are going to serve as its leaders must have their own houses in order! This qualification calls for both men of unique faith as well as women of the same quality. The home life of the elder became a picture as to how he will oversee the heritage of God. In this qualification of the home, we come into contact with the

---

[31] See Randall Justin Imel, "Shepherding Wandering Sheep: An Examination of Elder's Attitudes Regarding Inactive Christians" (D. Min. Dissertation, Regions University, 2007); Stephen Johnson, "A Narrative Model For Forming Pastoral Leaders At The Edgemere Church of Christ" (D. Min. Thesis, Abilene Christian University, 2000); Douglass B. Peters, "Selecting Spiritual Leaders: Spiritual Discernment and the Selection of Church Leaders At the North Davis Church of Christ" (D. Min. Thesis, Abilene Christian University, 2006); Douglas Leon Hall, "A Road Map For The Shepherds At Meadowlark Church of Christ" (D. Min. Thesis, Abilene Christian University, 2005).

[32] Alexander Strauch, *Biblical Eldership: Restoring The Eldership To Its Rightful Place in The Church* (Littleton, CO: Lewis & Roth Publishers, 1997), 17.

[33] See Julia P. Craig-Horne, "Pew to the Pulpit," 11.

[34] 1 Timothy 3:2; Titus 1:6.

[35] 1 Timothy 3:4.

concepts of fairness, discipline, respect, openness, understanding, problem solving and spiritual development. If
one wants to know whether a man has the ability to run the
church, just go visit the man's house and observe how his
family interacts and respects him. See if he is a tyrant or a
bully to his wife and children? Do they submit to his headship? Do they follow his lead and do they manifest a godly
attitude towards the spiritual direction of his lead?[36]

Elders are leaders with important responsibilities following
after the husband in the family. Everett Ferguson wisely writes:

> As the husband in the family exercises a leadership of love,
> so in the church its elders acting as stewards of God's house-
> hold exercise a loving, serving leadership following the
> example of Jesus (Matt. 20:25-28; John 13:1-17; 1 Peter
> 5:2-4). God's ranking of male and female going back to the
> creation and fall is reflected in males taking the leadership
> in the assembly and females following this leadership in
> respectful silence.[37]

Elders care for the spiritual well-being of the members.
According to Lugo[38], the work of elders includes: watching[39],
admonishing[40], feeding and tending the flock[41], ruling or
guiding[42], maturing the church[43], visiting and praying for the
sick[44], and overseeing[45].

---

[36] Luis R. Lugo, *The Five Fold Work of the Elder* (Homewood, IL: L&L
Publication, 2006) 79-80.

[37] Everett Ferguson, *Women in the Church*, 60.

[38] Luis R. Lugo, *The Five Fold Wok of the Evangelist*, 46.

[39] Acts 20:28-31.

[40] 2 Thessalonians 3:6-15.

[41] 1 Peter 5:1-5; Acts 20:28.

[42] Hebrews 13:17, 24; 1 Timothy 5:20.

[43] Ephesians 4:11.

[44] James 5:13-18.

[45] 1 Peter 5:1.

African American Churches of Christ are experiencing difficulties with elders because they are experiencing difficulties with their families. Harold R. Redd asserts that ministering to the African American family is one of the greatest challenges facing the African American church in the next century.[46] Redd also expresses concern for the African American male when he writes:

> A major concern for the black family is the plight of the black male. Black families must reclaim black males from prison cells and diseased communities that led them there, and the church must take part in that reclamation process.[47]

Others agree that there are serious concerns about the African American family and male in particular. Psychology Professors Derald Wing Sue and David Sue assert some have perhaps in a dehumanizing manner described the African-American male as an endangered species due to a higher mortality rate than white males.[48] Furthermore, slavery undermined the role of the African-American husband and hindered his ability to provide for his family and protect them.[49] Wilma A. Dunaway, while Associate Professor of Sociology at Virginia Polytechnic Institute and State University, describes the structured absence of the slave husband and father.[50] Dunaway asserts that the slave marriage had no legal rights.[51] Additionally, white slave masters often broke up slave families through sales. Wilma Dunaway writes:

> When Thomas Jefferson died, the families of 130 slaves were permanently separated. The five days of auctioning

---

[46] Harold R. Redd, "Leadership Training," 34.

[47] Ibid, 34.

[48] Derald Wing Sue & David Sue, *Counseling the Culturally Diverse: Theory and Practice 5th Edition* (Hoboken, New Jersey: John Wiley & Sons, Inc., 2008), 191.

[49] Ibid, 191.

[50] Wilma A. Dunaway, The African-American Family in Slavery and Emancipation (New York, NY: Cambridge University Press, 2003), 54.

[51] Ibid, 65.

were so traumatic that it reminded one of Jefferson's grand-children of "a captured village in ancient times when all were sold as slaves."[52]

Several factors contributed to the disempowerment of the African-American slave husband and father. In many cases, the husband and father did not live with the wife and children.[53] The slave master restricted the male slave's contact with his family often only allowing a weekly visit.[54] The children lived with the mother in her house.[55] The slave father did not usually discipline the slave children.[56] The slave children were considered the property of the mother's master[57] indicated by wearing the master's surname.[58]

The plight of the African American context has struck a blow against the family. In many cases, the African-American male is disadvantaged in comparison to the African American female. In one of the many illustrative articles in *The Covenant*,[59] David M. Satcher, Interim President of the Morehouse School of Medicine and former Surgeon General of the United States, writes:

> There are also gender differences among African-Americans that relate to income gains experienced by African-American women and the provision of Medicaid, which is more amenable to black women than to black men. Violence and gun related deaths have taken a toll on African American men. Disproportionate numbers of black men

---

[52] Ibid, 59.

[53] Ibid, 61.

[54] Ibid, 61.

[55] Ibid, 64.

[56] Ibid, 64.

[57] Ibid, 64.

[58] Ibid, 65.

[59] *The Covenant* addresses the challenges and problems of African American life and presents practical and responsible actions for African Americans to take. Among the problems and concerns are housing, education, racial profiling, health care, and injustice.

are incarcerated as a result of policies that mandate imprisonment as opposed to treatment for substance abuse.[60]

Furthermore, Paulette Moore Hines and Nancy Boyd-Franklin describe this disparity concerning gender roles and couple relationships of African-Americans. Hine and Boyd-Franklin write:

African-American women, who are often more actively religious than their mates, are frequently regarded as the "strength of the family." More easily employed than their male counterparts, Black women historically have worked outside the home, sometimes as the sole wage earners, particularly in times of high unemployment.[61]

The Church cannot have elders without having African-American men that are leading their families with godly headship. Slavery has influenced the African-American experience. Slavery adversely affected the family. William Lynch, a white slave owner in the 1700s, describes his psychological methods of 'breaking slaves:'

Pay little attention to the generation of original breaking, but concentrate on future generations. Therefore, if you break the female mother, she will break the offspring in its early years of development and, when the offspring is old enough to work, she will deliver it up to you for her normal female protective tendencies will have been lost in the original breaking process.[62]

Lynch also compared African slaves to horses to be bred and broken when he writes:

---

[60] David M. Satcher, "Securing the Right to Healthcare and Well-Being," in *The Covenant*, ed. Tavis Smiley (Chicago, IL: Third World Press, 2006), 5.

[61] Paulette Moore Hines & Nancy Boyd-Franklin, "African American Families," in *Ethnicity & Family Therapy 3rd Edition*, eds. Monica McGoldrick, Joe Giordano, & Nydia Garcia-Preto (New York, NY: Guilford Press, 2005), 90.

[62] The Willie Lynch Letter And The Making of A Slave. Published by Lushena Books in Bensenville, IL: 1999, 14.

Take the meanest and most restless nigger, strip him of his clothes in front of the remaining male niggers, the female, and the nigger infant, tar and feather him, tie each leg to a different horse in opposite directions, set him a fire and beat both horses to pull him apart in front of the remaining niggers. The next step is to take a bullwhip and beat the remaining nigger male to the point of death in front of the female and infant. Don't kill him, but put the fear of God in him, for he can be useful for future breeding.[63]

Lynch describes the process of breaking the African woman when he writes:

In this frozen psychological state of independence she will raise her male and female offspring in reversed roles. For fear of the young male's life, she will psychologically train him to be mentally weak and dependent but physically strong. Because she has become psychologically independent, she will train her female offspring's to be psychologically independent. What have you got? You've got the nigger woman out front and the man behind and scared. This is a perfect situation for sound sleep and economics.[64]

Furthermore, Lynch describes the assault against the family when he writes:

Continually, though the breaking of uncivilized savage niggers, by throwing the nigger female savage into a frozen psychological state of independency, by killing of the protective male image by creating a submissive dependent mind of the nigger male savage, we have created an orbiting cycle that turns in its own axis forever, unless a phenomenon occurs and reshifts the positions of the female savages."[65]

---

[63] Ibid, 15.
[64] Ibid, 17.
[65] Ibid, 17.

Lynch's comments on the marriage unit or reproduction process are quite relevant to this issue. Lynch writes:

We breed two nigger males with two nigger females. Then we take the nigger males from them and keep them moving and working. Say the one nigger female bear a nigger female and the other bears a nigger male. Both nigger females, being without the influence of the nigger image, frozen with an independent psychology, will raise their offspring into reverse positions. The one with the female offspring will teach her to be like herself, independent and negotiable (we negotiate with her, through her, by her and negotiate her at will). The one with the nigger male offspring, she being frozen with a subconscious fear for his life, will raise him to be mentally dependent and weak, but physically strong- in other words, body over mind. Now in a few years when these two offspring become fertile for early reproduction, we will make and breed them and continue the cycle. That is good, sound, and long range comprehensive planning.[66]

Although greatly improved, the impact of slavery on the African American family continues to damage leadership potential. While serving as Alphonse Fletcher, Jr. Professor at Harvard University, Cornell West describes the present crisis of black leadership when he writes:

Presently, black communities are in shambles, black families are in decline, and black men and women are in conflict (and sometimes combat).[67]

Since many African American 'families are in decline,' it makes it more challenging to develop men to serve as elders. It took the

[66] Ibid, 19.
[67] Cornell West, *Race Matters* (New York, NY: Vintage Books, 1993), 56.

Northwest Church of Christ twenty-seven years to ordain elders because there was not a plurality of qualified men desiring the work.

Deacons

Deacons are servants in the church.[68] Ferguson asserts that deacons serve under the elders;[69] Strauch believes deacons have authority along with elders,[70] and Lugo claims deacons serve under both the evangelist and elders.[71] Common areas of responsibility for deacons include: benevolence, finances, education, maintenance, and whatever is necessary for the growth of the church.[72] Although the qualification to be the husband of one wife would exclude women from assuming the official role of deacon, some do argue the point.[73] Everett Ferguson calls it 'an open question' when he writes:

> It is an open question whether women were recognized for their services to the church as female deacons. Romans 16:1-2 says of Phoebe, "I commend to you our sister Phoebe, a servant [diakonos, deacon] of the church at Cenchreae, … for she has been a benefactor of many and of myself as well." A benefactor or patron(ess) was a person with resources who provided for others and received duties from them in return. Since the predominant use of diakonos in the New Testament is as general term and only seldom as a technical term for an appointed and representative servant of the church (as in Phil. 1:1 and 1 Tim. 3:8), it may be too much (although possible) to claim the latter meaning

---

[68] The term deacon means servant. Luis R. Lugo, *The Five Fold Work of the Evangelist*, 56.

[69] Everett Ferguson, *Women in the Church*, 9.

[70] Alexander Strauch, "Women Deacons, Deacons Assistants, or Wives of Deacons?," *Emmaus Journal* Volume 1 (1992): 196-214.

[71] Luis R. Lugo, *The Five Fold Work of the Evangelist*, 57.

[72] Ibid, 57.

[73] 1 Timothy 3:12.

for Phoebe. First Timothy 3:11, on the other hand, has a better claim to refer to women deacons, but the meanings "wives" or (less likely) "women servants" cannot be ruled out. The position of deacon (=servant) was a serving role.[74]

Others claim the reality of female deacons in early church history. H. Wayne House writes:

The office of deaconess is not certain in the New Testament church, but the preponderance of evidence suggests that women had this ministry, for it is certainly seen in the postapostolic period.[75]

Still others like Alexander Strauch argue against ordaining women to the office of deacon.[76] Strauch asserts that the three common interpretations of 1 Timothy 3:11 are women deacons, deacons' assistants, and wives of deacons.[77] Although Strauch makes his argument based on his perceived notion of deacon authority, others do agree with the conclusion that the role of deacon is limited to men.[78]

Women

If women cannot serve as evangelists, elders and deacons, then what options do they have for ministry? John Jefferson Davis, while Assistant Professor of Theology at Gordon-Conwell Theological Seminary captures the nature of the present problem when he writes:

---

[74] Everett Ferguson, *Women in the Church*, 9.

[75] H. Wayne House, *"A Biblical View of Women in the Ministry: Part 4 The Ministry of Women in the Apostolic and Postapostolic Periods,"* Bibliotheca Sacra Volume 145 (1988): 391.

[76] Alexander Strauch, Women Deacons, Deacons' Assistants, or Wives of Deacons?, 196-214.

[77] Ibid.

[78] Lugo, when describing deacons mentions men only. Luis R. Lugo, *The Five Fold Work of the Evangelist*, 58.

In our own contemporary situation, we are likewise faced with increasing confusion about our role identities as men and women. For the past two centuries, the process of industrialization and urbanization has moved the populations of the West from the farms, with their relatively clear and traditional role identities, into the increasingly bureaucratized cities, where traditional identities have become eroded. The recent impact of the feminist movement, the pressure for the equal rights amendment, and the gay liberation movement have called into question traditional understandings of sexual roles as well as their Biblical and theological foundations. There is much uncertainty, both inside and outside of the Church, about what it means to be a man or a woman in our contemporary situation. The proper roles of men and women in marriage and family, in the Church, and in the wider society are the subject of an ongoing debate that has touched us all.[79]

The Inspired writers of the New Testament appealed to creation when it came to the role of women in the Church.[80] Neil R. Lightfoot, a prominent Christian scholar, writes:

It is interesting that in each case where women are forbidden to speak or teach in church, Paul appeals to the original created order and what the law says. His arguments are based, not on custom but on Old Testament Scripture.[81]

When applying the New Testament principles, Lightfoot describes the limitations of women in the Church when he writes:

---

[79] John Jefferson Davis, "Some Reflections on Galatians 3:28, Sexual Roles, and Biblical Hermeneutics," *Journal of the Evangelical Theological Society* Volume 19 (1976): 202.

[80] 1 Timothy 2:13-15; 1 Corinthians 14:35.

[81] Neil R. Lightfoot, *The Role of Women: The New Testament Perspectives*, (Memphis, TN: Mercury Printing, 1978), 37.

Women in the assembly are to learn in all submissiveness, and they are not to teach men. Otherwise, how could the woman teach, or preside in the meeting, and still be subject to one of the members in the meeting, her husband?[82]

In response to those claiming female liberation based on Galatians 3:28, Ferguson writes:

Just as a person in Christ continues to be a Jew or a Gentile, slave or free, so one does not cease being male or female. Unlike slavery, a changeable human institution, but like being born a Jew or a Gentile, a person's gender is not subject to change (not naturally—that one can undergo a sex change operation does not affect the argument here any more than does a Gentile becoming circumcised or a Jew having an operation to remove his circumcision). The normal biological, psychological, and sociological differences between male and female remain, and so do the regulations pertaining to their different roles (Eph. 5:22-33).[83]

Christian women in the New Testament were able to make significant contributions while being restricted from certain roles. Ferguson asserts that in the New Testament women prophesied[84], taught[85], helped to advance the Gospel[86], performed unspecified work[87], performed hospitality and served as benefactors[88], and certain qualified widows served the church[89].[90]

---

[82] Ibid, 39.

[83] Everett Ferguson, *Women in the Church*, 67.

[84] Acts 2:17-18; Acts 21:9; 1 Corinthians 11:5.

[85] Acts 18:26; Titus 2:3-5.

[86] Philippians 4:3; Romans 16:7.

[87] Romans 6:6, 12.

[88] Acts 16:15, 40; Romans 16:2.

[89] 1 Timothy 5:3-16.

[90] Everett Ferguson, *Women in the Church*, 7-9.

There are many ministry opportunities for women.[91] However, Luis R. Lugo laments the failure of African-American Churches of Christ to utilize women in the work of the church. Lugo writes:

> Black women today are educated, trained and capable of doing things within the church that does not abuse nor disqualify men from their role in the church. Women are part of the body of Christ and should not be treated as second class members simply because there is a prohibition as to her place in teaching and authority over men in a public arena. Women today are aggressive and passionate about their contributions in the spiritual arena. The Lord's church must not miss this opportunity to utilize this resource. Women need to know that there is a place of ministry for them in the church. That their talents and abilities will be utilized in areas that bring about fulfillment and joy in ministries.[92]

Ann L. Bowman, while Assistant Professor of Biblical Studies at International School of Theology, proposed a number of ministry opportunities for women based on their spiritual gifts. Bowman includes as opportunities for women to take various teaching roles such as Sunday school, Vacation Bible School, Children's church, Neighborhood Bible Studies, Youth Director, Director of Christian Education, Director of Women's ministries, Curriculum Development, Writing, and Workplace Bible Studies. Other opportunities, according to Bowman, include visitation programs, Retirement Home ministries, Telephone Outreach Surveys, Conference Speaking, Counseling, Administrative assistant, Choirs, Meals on Wheels, Fellowship Dinners, Church Bus Driver, Pastoral Support staff, Home Bible Studies, Ministry

---

[91] See Wayne Grudem, "But what should women do in the church?" *Journal for Biblical Manhood and Womanhood* Volume 1 (1995).

[92] Luis R. Lugo, "The Church in Transition," *The Revivalist* (April-June 2008): 18.

to the sick and physically challenged, Prayer, Website Design, Creating Banners, Reporting to the local Newspaper, and Floral Arrangement.[93]

---

[93] Ann L. Bowman, "Women, Spiritual Gifts, and Ministry," *Faith and Mission* Volume 14 (1996): 69-70.

Lawrence W. Rodgers

Lawrence W. Rodgers is the Ministering Evangelist of the Westside Church of Christ in Baltimore, Maryland, and the author of blog SeekingFirst.org where he writes about relevant practical issues that Christians face in their everyday life. Lawrence is happily married to his wife Bettae and they recently had their first child in 2013. He has earned a degree in Bible/Ministry from Harding University and currently working on his graduate education in Divinity. Lawrence believes that a spiritual revival is upon the horizon and wants to be a part of that glorious occasion by way of preaching, and writing regarding the oracles of God, and the application thereof.

CHAPTER 12

Reaching the Millennial: Reclaiming a Lost Generation

Lawrence Rodgers

—ɯ—

Today's church faces several problems, but one of the most serious is asking the question: Where have all the Millennials/Mosaics gone? Millennials are people in the 18-30 age brackets, in other words, people born between 1983 and the early 2000s.[94] The Millennial/Mosaics are one of the largest generations in America. However, if one were to visit congregations around the country they would observe that members of the millennial generation are just not there. On the other hand, if you go to a congregation containing a healthy number of Mosaics (another term for this demographic) you are most likely in a college town, or some other unique situation.

---

[94] Marino, Vivian (2006-08-20). "College-Town Real Estate: The Next Big Niche?". *The New York Times* (The New York Times Company). p. 1.

Statistically if your congregation is like the average congregation then Millennials are rare. According to The Barna Group, a leading church researcher, roughly ¼ of the Mosaic generation practices Christianity which translates to one church service a month.[95] If that number is startling to you then let me also add: "59 percent of young people with a Christian background report that they had or have 'dropped out of attending church, after going regularly.' A majority (57 percent) say they are less active in church today compared to when they were age fifteen. Nearly two-fifths (38 percent) say they have gone through a period when they significantly doubted their faith. Another one-third (32 percent) describe a period when they felt like rejecting their parents' faith." [96] I am concerned that church leaders are not addressing these issues proactively, resulting in too many of them simply watching the church in America die.

Some may think it is impossible for the church to die in America. However, to such a person I would point to the United Kingdom, which, use to be the epicenter of Christianity, but now churches find themselves on an increasing decline for over a decade.[97] For instance, in London exists the Metropolitan Tabernacle, which was once pastored by Charles Haddon Spurgeon. Under his ministry, the church had thousands in attendance and had to issue tickets to get in due to crowds exceeding seating capacity. Now the church only has a few hundred in attendance.

---

[95] Barna Group, "5 Reasons Millennials Stay Connected to Church," Accessed January 6, 2014, https://www.barna.org/barna-update/millennials/635-5-reasons-millennials-stay-connected-to-church#.Uq1tiZGwBXp

[96] David Kinnaman and Aly Hawkins, *You Lost Me: Why Young Christians Are Leaving Church ... and Rethinking Faith* (Grand Rapids, MI: Baker Books, 2011), 23.

[97] International Business Times, "Christianity Is In Decline And Could Go Extinct In The UK, Says Lord George Carey," Accessed January 6, 2014, http://www.ibtimes.com/christianity-decline-could-go-extinct-uk-says-lord-george-carey-1477466

In America, the percentage of those outside of Christianity is growing with each generation. For instance among ages 61+ only 23 percent are outside of Christianity while 77 percent identify as Christians. By comparison those aged 42-50 has 27 percent outside and 73 percent identify themselves as Christians, in the 18-41 age bracket 37 percent are outside and 63 percent identify as Christians, and finally those 16-29 are 40 percent outside of Christianity with only 60 percent within Christianity.[98] Some might say that 63 percent is still a majority, but if we dig deeper into the numbers, we will see that many of those who claim to be Christians do not ever attend a regular Christian assembly service. Out of those numbers, no more than 20 percent of Millennials attend church once a month or more. This means that if one takes the traditional view that faith happens in a community, and therefore part of being a Christian is regularly attending church services, then it means that while Millenials represent the largest generation in America's history with almost 80 million members, only 15% are Christians.[99]

I would encourage the readers to look at the demographics of your own congregation. Granted, some churches have made serious attempts to reach out to Millennials and often their sowing reaps them a bountiful harvest; but the congregations who have done nothing to reach out to the Millennial generation will find this statistic to ring true.

According to researcher Barna.org there are three groups in the 18-29 age bracket that would be considered spiritually home-less youth: The Nomads, The Prodigals, and The Exiles. Before we go into those three distinctions, some general things about the

[98] Barna Group, "A New Generation Expresses its Skepticism and Frustration with Christianity," Accessed January 6, 2014, https://www.barna.org/barna-update/teens-nextgen/94-a-new-generation-expresses-its-skepticism-and-frus-tration-with-christianity#.UrHPE5GwBXo

[99] ThomRainer.com, "Six Ways Millennials Are Shaping the Church," Accessed January 6, 2014, http://thomrainer.com/2013/12/11/six-ways-millennials-are-shaping-the-church/

spiritually homeless youth is that fifty-nine percent of them have dropped out of attending church after previously going regularly. Also, fifty percent have been significantly frustrated by their faith, and another thirty eight percent went through a period when they significantly doubted their faith.

The first distinction among the three groups is the Nomads. Nomads have a Christian background and consider themselves Christians, but have walked away from church engagement. Among Nomads, forty three percent think going to church or being with Christian friends is optional. Twenty five percent say that faith and religion are just not that important to them right now. Twenty three percent say they used to be very involved in their church but do not feel they fit anymore. The second group is called The Prodigals. They have a Christian background but have lost their faith, and describe themselves as "no longer Christian." Out of this group twenty percent say they had a negative experience in church or with Christians. Twenty-one percent say Christian beliefs just don't make sense to them while nineteen percent say their spiritual needs cannot be met by Christianity. The last group is the Exiles, who have a Christian background and are still invested in their Christian faith but feel stuck (or lost) between culture and the church. Out of this group thirty eight percent say they want to find a way to follow Jesus that connects with the world they live in. Thirty three percent say God is more at work outside the church than inside and they want to be a part of that. Thirty percent say they want to be a Christian without separating themselves from the world around them.[100]

Unfortunately, when many church leaders are asked about the lack of Millennials in their congregation they respond by attempting to place the burden and responsibility on the fallen away. Granted

---

[100] Barna Group, "Three Spiritual Journeys of Millennials ," Accessed January 6, 2014, https://www.barna.org/barna-update/millennials/612-three-spiritual-journeys-of-millennials.html#exiles

they do have a responsibility, however it does not completely fall on them. In order to reach those in each of these groups, we must look at the specific characteristics that define them. Regarding the Nomads the church must ask why are these people not in attendance. Well, twenty five percent of them say that they do not fit in at church anymore. Armed with that information, the church must ask are they doing anything to make them feel at home? Are there any young adult ministries? Are there any college ministries? How about the songs we sing, are there any contemporary hymns in the mix with traditional hymns, or are all the songs from the late 1800s and early 1900s? When a church ignores their concerns questions, it says to a young person that the church does not care about whether they have a place, and that the assembly exists solely for old people, and not the young. Is this the message we should send? Another twenty five percent of Nomads says faith and religion is just not important to them anymore. Often church leaders will say that the lack of Millennials in the church is due to apathy. However, let me add that the other volunteer organizations such as the American Red Cross, Peace Corps, Greenpeace, or AmeriCorps are not having trouble enlisting Millennials. Then why does the church have problems? Maybe it is because the church herself has either lost or failed to communicate her mission to love God with all her heart, soul, mind, and strength; and secondly to love her neighbor as self. If Millennials received the same commitment from us that Jesus had to those who were marginalized, poor, and suffering, then maybe they would find faith and religion important to them and the world that they live in.

The next group is The Prodigals who grew up in the Christianity but have lost their faith, and describe themselves as "no longer Christians." Now, this is the group that I have a particular affinity because it is a shame for anyone to lose their faith. I grew up in the church and can personally attest to two conversations taking place. The young generation has been under attack not only in their school system, but also in academia. Secular academics have been taught not just to have a neutral position on the supernatural, but are actually hostile towards faith, or anything loosely related to faith or a creator such as intelligent design. To add reinforcement the "Four Horsemen of New Atheism": Richard Dawkins, Sam Harris, Daniel C. Dennet, and Christopher Hitchens have philosophically hijacked the mind of many professors in state colleges and universities. An after effect of this is that the messages of these New York Times bestselling atheist author(s) is that it has bled into pop culture through popular television shows such as Family Guy, and South Park to name just a few. These four horsemen have written many books such as the *God Delusion, God Is Not Great,* and *A Letter to a Christian Nation.* Millennials are being assigned these books by their professors and pressured to accept such ideas by their peers and mainstream media. Unfortunately, the church's response was not an apologetics discussion. Unfortunately, too many congregations have been focused on defending their style of Sunday morning assembly service while neglecting the weightier matters such as cultivating the faith of her young people.

The second thing I would like to point out about The Prodigals is that twenty percent say that they experienced a negative experience in the church that contributed to them losing their faith. I can identify with negative experiences in the church. The nastiest I have every seen church members treated was not from the world, but from other church people. Also, too many members of the church consider their citizenship in the world to be greater than their citizenship in Heaven. Therefore, politics, bigotry, sexism, ageism, racism, chauvinism and all types of ideologies that are counter to the will of God, and the way of Jesus can been found in many congregations. When Millennials see these things in the church it reeks of hypocrisy, causing them to be put off over the idea that these individuals are the "people of God." Granted the people of God have always had issues, which is why we need a Savior. However, this is no excuse for us to refuse to attempt to improve ourselves by lifting up Christ in our lives, ideas, thoughts, and ways, thereby drawing all men and women including Millennials to him.

The next group is the Exiles who are eighteen- to twenty-nine-year-olds with a Christian background and still invested in their Christian faith, but they feel stuck (or lost) between culture and the church. Looking across your congregation on the average Sunday morning you will notice that any Millennials you have will more than likely be within this group called Exiles. They are there, but they are not invested. Often times they are, they are simply trying to appease the desires of a dear loved one. However, when this group is mobilized they can transform the congregation, the city, and even the world, but mobilizing them will only come by being willing to invest in their faith and spirituality.

There are a few facts about the Exile generation that are important to know. *Exiles are not inclined to being separate from "the world."*[101] Exiles want their faith to matter, and want it to engage the world they live in. They want to be sanctified, but sent. *"They are skeptical of institutions but are not wholly disengaged from them"*[8] Exiles are leery of institutions for a reason. They have seen, read about, or studied about the harm that intuitions created by men and women can do. Therefore, when corruption and hypocrisy are found in the church it is especially offensive to Millennials. *"Young exiles sense God moving 'outside the walls of the church.'"*[8] Many who still subscribe to the idol worship of church buildings may fail to realize that Jesus calls us to ministry outside the walls of the building: this shortcoming is frustrating to Exiles. Many Exiles are confused when traditionalist, and legalists argue over liturgical practices. To them that is the smallest sliver of the pie, what about Matthew 25:31-46, or Mark 12:28-31? *"They are not disillusioned with tradition; they are frustrated with slick or shallow expressions of*

---

[101] David Kinnaman and Aly Hawkins, *You Lost Me: Why Young Christians Are Leaving Church ... and Rethinking Faith* (Grand Rapids, MI: Baker Books, 2011), 77.

religion." [8] Exiles desire a real, genuine, organic faith that is not covered in lights or facades, but genuine, I love the Lord, therefore I serve him, and serve my neighbor. Exiles also want things to make sense. They dislike doing something just for the sake of doing it, and therefore tradition for the sake of tradition seems disingenuous. "*They have not found faith to be instructive to their calling or gifts.*" [8] This is truly sad because as the Bible clearly articulates in 1 Corinthians 12:12-27, all the parts of the body are needed. So, it can be quite sobering for both male and female Exiles when they cannot find some way to use their God given gifts to serve God within the community of faith.

The Exile group is a group that the church can focus on right now, and use them to reach the Nomads, and possibly the Prodigals. However, if this group is ignored, if there is not an effort put forth to actively reach out to the Millennial/Mosaic Generation then we will continue to lose them to the world. Some simple things that can be done to help encourage cross-generational outreach at your congregation are: 1) preaching inductively, 2) adding contemporary Christian songs to your congregational singing, 3) young adult small groups and fellowship ministries, 4) mentoring programs between older members and young members, such as adopt a student, 5) campus ministries and other outreach tools, 6) not being afraid to deal with the tough topics.

In order to reach not just Millennials/Mosaics, but for the sake of reaching everyone Christians must learn to grow out of legalism. It is not appealing and makes no sense when you read the teachings of Jesus, or the Apostle Paul, especially from Galatians and Romans. As Kinnaman and Lyons write, "The real problem comes when we recognize God's holiness but fail to articulate the other side of his character: grace. Jesus represents truth *plus* grace (see John 1:14). Embracing truth without holding grace in tension leads to harsh legalism, just as grace without truth devolves to compromise. Still, the important insight based on our research is that Mosaics and Busters rarely see Christians who embody service, compassion, humility, forgiveness, patience, kindness, peace, joy, goodness, and love." [102] People are looking for a house of grace, a house of redemption, not a house of condemnation or hypocrisy, for as Paul writes in Romans 8:1-2: "There is therefore now no condemnation for those who are in Christ Jesus. ² For the law of the Spirit of life has set you free in Christ Jesus from the law of sin and death." [103] What Christians often forget is that the assembly service is supposed to be a house of encouragement.[104] Don't we all need encouragement in this rather discouraging world full of sin and temptation? Christians need to get back to studying and proclaiming the weightier matters of the law, such as justice, mercy, and faithfulness. This kind of assembly and community will not only be appealing to Mosaics but to everyone. It only makes sense because as Jesus told us, if He be lifted up he will draw all men and women to himself.

This chapter of this book is a call to all who read it to take the ministry of outreach to the Millennial/Mosaic generation seriously, as if the future of the church in this world depends on it.

Thanks for Reading!

~ Lawrence W. Rodgers

---

[102] David Kinnaman and Gabe Lyons, *UnChristian: What a New Generation Really Thinks About Christianity ... and Why It Matters* (Grand Rapids, MI: Baker Books, 2007), 36-37.

[103] *The Holy Bible: English Standard Version* (Wheaton: Standard Bible Society, 2001), Rom. 8:1-2.

[104] See Hebrews 10:25

Ronald N. Wearing

Ronald N. Wearing is married with two teenage daughters. He received his Bachelor of Science degree in mathematics and education from Clemson University. He received his Masters of Arts degree in Educational Leadership from Furman University in Greenville, SC. He also has obtained an Education Specialist degree from Argosy University in Sarasota, Florida. He is certified as an administrator in elementary, middle and high school levels. Ronald has been an administrator in the School District of Pickens County for the last eleven years. He is a former school teacher of middle and high school students. Bro. Wearing grew up in the Andrews Church of Christ, where he learned the art of teaching Bible classes and delivered his first sermon at twelve years old. He has served as the minister of the William St. Church of Christ in Seneca, SC for the past twenty-one years. Brother Wearing is passionately called "the teacher" because of his teaching ministry.

He believes:

... That the word of God has the Power to transform lives... Rom. 12:2

...God's has two great institutions the family and the church... Eph. 5

...God expects us to Grow and develop ourselves... Heb. 5:12-13

...We serve God by serving others Matt. 25: 32-46

Chapter 13

Transitioning from Boys to Men: A Failure Effect on Church Leadership

Ronald Wearing

—⁓—

1 Corinthians 13:11: When I was a child, I spake as a child, I understood as a child, I thought as a child: but when I became a man, I put away childish things.

Introduction

Do we in the church have a pool of qualified men who are ready for leadership? Do we have faithful men to commit the word of God that will teach others as well? Can we follow Paul's charge to Titus and ordain elders (or deacons) in every congregation? Do we have men with a desire to become leaders in the church?

The answers to these questions will vary depending upon a number of circumstances. To some congregations the answer is "yes" and to others, "no." Most would agree that the answer should be yes to all. Then why is it not yes?

Leadership issues in our churches are impacted by leadership issues in our homes. Leadership in the home has to deal with healthy husband and wife relationships. Leadership in the home also depends on positive father and children relationships. Leadership, likewise, is contingent on biblical characteristics of manhood.

These characteristics are developed during the transformation from being a boy to becoming a man. First Corinthians 13:11 states "When I was a child, I spoke as a child, I understood as a child, I thought as a child: but when I became a man, I put away childish things." If this transformation is successful, then the seeds of leadership are being planted. However, a failure in this transformation can and will cause an effect on a man's leadership ability in the home, community and the church.

Changing Society

American society has changed so much over the past one-hundred years. We have shifted from an Agrarian (farming) based society to an industrial (mills) based, to now a technology society. These changes in our society have included many positive improvements in and to family life. The average family has many comforts that were never imagined only three or four generations ago. These changes have also brought a number of negatives. The change that we will focus on for this context is the quantity and quality of family time, especially that of fathers and sons.

The family has always been God's system for the transmission values. Consider Moses' charge to the children of Israel in Deuteronomy 6:2 "fear the LORD thy God, to keep all His statutes and His commandments, which I command thee, thou, and thy son, and thy son's son, all the days of thy life." These values were to be passed on through all the successive generations. From biblical days until the last one-hundred years, most families had a farm. On the farm, the parents and children would work together to provide for the family. This time of working together was the method of passing on values and culture.

As a father and son(s) were working, to pass the time talking and teaching was a common occurrence. While I did not grow up on a farm, my parents did. We planted almost a full acre of vegetables. We would have to prepare the land (plow), plant the seeds, water the seeds, hoe the young plants to remove the grass, and then harvest the vegetables. This entire process allowed for a great deal of time together. Moses' command to the parents of Israel in Deuteronomy 6:7 "thou shalt teach them diligently unto thy children, and shalt talk of them when thou sittest in thine house, and when thou walkest by the way, and when thou liest down, and when thou risest up."

During these work sessions, my father would talk to my brother and me about the issues that arose in the community, especially those that dealt with being a **_real man_**. Real men issues included topics like being a man versus acting like a boy; true manhood is not just having a baby. It is how a husband should treat his wife, how fathers should treat their children and how to be a leader in the community.

In recent years, more and more fathers began to work in mills and other industrial settings. Many fathers would work second shift or third shift. This would lead to them spending less and less time with their sons. Additionally, the other factor is that numerous people have moved from the rural areas to the urban environment. In most rural settings, a family was surrounded by extended family members or friends of the family that share similar values. In the urban environment, you may have countless neighbors who share a totally different set of values.

True Manhood

The concept of manhood or being a MAN has varied over the years and in different cultures and sub-cultures. This variation may range from a male that possess high qualities, such as character and courage, to a male who can fight and produce many babies. These differences in definitions depend on the values of the groups defining manhood. For example, those from a conservative background would define manhood by character qualities. Those who live in a survival environment would define manhood by a male who could fight and protect them. Therefore, we need to define this concept of "True Manhood" both legally and biblically.

According to Merriam-Webster's dictionary, manhood is defined as: 1) an adult male, 2) the state or condition of being an adult man and no longer a boy and 3) the qualities (such as strength and courage) that are expected in a man.

This first definition of manhood is listed as an adult male; a male is considered an adult at the age of eighteen to twenty-one. There are a number of physical changes that some would use to consider a male as reaching manhood. For example, the male's physical size, facial hairs or the ability to reproduce are factors. There are many males who have reached these chronological landmarks, but not the maturity that is expected of men.

In some American sub-cultures a test of manhood is having children with multiple women. Some males will boast of the number of children they have fathered illegitimately. This is **false manhood;** however our young boys see example after example of this activity. Because of the enormous number of negative models, many boys truly believe that this is what being a man is about.

This second definition considers the process of moving from boyhood to manhood. This is aligned with our biblical text of 1 Corinthians 13:11 "When I was a child, I spake as a child, I understood as a child, I thought as a child: but when I became a man, I put away childish things."

I enjoyed my youth significantly. I played football, baseball and basketball both on the playground and on formal teams. As a boy,

I rode my bicycle all over my small town. I spent summer days playing with my brother and sisters and many cousins. Hopefully, many of you also have similar memories of your youth. Back then, life was simple and carefree for a boy. Then I grew up, married a wife, got car payments and a mortgage. Now, my life includes children, insurance and braces. As a man, I cannot return to playing ball (video games) all day. I must act as a man and handle my responsibilities.

The process of moving from a boy to a man was aided by my father's guidance. In the midst of those carefree days, my parents began to teach values that as you grow, there are more responsibilities in life. As we grew, playtime became work time. There were conversations about acquiring things (possessions) in life and what as a man I should strive to achieve. A popular verse quoted in our home was 2 Thessalonians 3:10 …"that if any would not work, neither should he eat."

The third definition contemplates the character qualities of manhood. My childhood minister taught many lessons on manhood. He used Genesis 2:15 -18 to describe when a male was man enough to have a woman.

Genesis 2:15 And the LORD God took the man, and put him into the Garden of Eden to dress it and to keep it. And the LORD God commanded the man, saying, Of every tree of the garden thou mayest freely eat: But of the tree of the knowledge of good and evil, thou shalt not eat of it: for in the day that thou eatest thereof thou shalt surely die. And the LORD God said, It is not good that the man should be alone; I will make him an help meet for him.

There were three points he would stress: 1) a man first needed a job, 2) secondly, he needed a home and 3) thirdly, he should have a relationship with God. If you consider the Genesis text, Adam has a job to dress and keep the Garden of Eden (verse 15). His home was the Garden of Eden (verse 15). Also, God gave him the law of what should and should not be eaten (verses 16 and 17). This is the test of "True Manhood," not males boasting of the number of children they have fathered illegitimately.

Husband and Wife

How a young man treats his wife is inspired by the models he has viewed growing up. Many of our boys and young men have not been exposed to positive marriage models. The number of boys growing up without their biological father is at an all-time high. These young men have witnessed the examples of false manhood mentioned earlier. Case in point, a teenage boy looks up to a very popular male figure in the community who is known as a "player." This male has no wife, but five children with four different "baby mammas." This so-called player still lives either with his own mother or moves from one "baby mamma" to another "baby mamma." This teenager will most likely follow the only models that are available to him.

Young men need to be exposed to more biblical examples of positive husband and wife relationships. This exposure begins by examining God's word on husband and wife relationships. In Matthew 19:4 Jesus said unto them, "Have ye not read, that he which made them at the beginning made them male and female, And said, For this cause shall a man leave father and mother, and shall cleave to his wife: and they twain shall be one flesh? Wherefore they are no more twain, but one flesh. What therefore God hath joined together, let not man put asunder."

God's pattern for a healthy marriage is one man and one woman in a committed marriage for life. As more and more young men understand God's requirement for them to become committed in their relationships, they are prepared themselves to become committed to other leadership roles.

God's arrangement also states how a husband should treat his wife. A lot of young men in today's society have viewed count-less negative scenes of men mistreating women, even their own mothers. Much of today's popular music is very hostile toward females. These are all examples of false manhood and they can hinder the proper transitioning from boyhood to manhood. We will share some statistics on domestic violence in America:

- One in four women (25%) has experienced domestic violence in her lifetime. [1]

- Women accounted for 85% of the victims of intimate partner violence.[2]

- Women of all races are about equally vulnerable to violence by an intimate partner.[3]

- Intimate partner violence affects people regardless of income. However, people with lower annual income (below $25K) are at a 3-times higher risk of intimate partner violence than people with higher annual income (over $50K).*[4]

- 30% of Americans say they know a woman who has been physically abused by her husband or boyfriend in the past year.[5]

- In 2000, 1,247 women were killed by an intimate partner.[6]

- Approximately one in five female high school students reports being physically and/or sexually abused by a dating partner.[7]

- One in five teens in a serious relationship reports having been hit, slapped, or pushed by a partner. 14% of teens report their boyfriend or girlfriend threatened to harm them or themselves to avoid a breakup.[8]

This is in vast contrast to God's vision of a husband's treatment of his wife. There are scriptural illustrations of the manner in which men need to treat their wives. In Ephesians chapter 5,

Paul states that "Husbands, love your wives, even as Christ also loved the church, and gave himself for it; That he might sanctify and cleanse it with the washing of water by the word, that he might present it to himself a glorious church, not having spot, or wrinkle, or any such thing; but that it should be holy and without blemish. So ought men to love their wives as their own bodies. He that loveth his wife loveth himself. For no man ever yet hated his own flesh; but nourisheth and cherisheth it, even as the Lord the church:" This passage implies that men should love by supporting and protecting their wives, and husbands should, if necessary, lay down their lives for their wives.

Father and Children

Earlier, we discussed changes in our society that have affected both the quantity and the quality of the time that fathers spend with their children and with their sons in particular. Data shows the prevalence of physical fatherlessness (the absent of a father), which affects more than 25 million children. Emotional fatherlessness—when dad is in the home, but not emotionally engaged with his child's life—affects millions more.

Boyz n the Hood is a 1991 American drama film written and directed by John Singleton. The movie is about a ten-year-old boy who lives with his single mother. Frightened about the future of her child, the mother sends him to live with his twenty-seven-year-old father. The father, who appears to be the only father present in the neighborhood, takes his son on fishing trips, where he advises his son to act mature, and be responsible when he becomes a father. The father provides structure and discipline and warns his son not to become involved in the street (gang) life. The movie fast forwards seven-years later and now all of the boys in the neighborhood are either in a gang, on drugs, in prison or dead. The boy has a number of tough choices, but survives to leave the neighborhood for college. His survival is in great part due to having his father very active in his life.

This movie, although very graphic in street violence, does show the effects of fatherlessness in America. Let us consider the following data on fatherlessness:

- Fatherlessness is the most significant family or social problem facing America according to 72.2 % of the U.S. population.[9]

- An estimated 24.35 million children (33.5 percent) live absent their biological father.[10]

- Children in father-absent homes are almost four times more likely to be poor. In 2011, 12 percent of children in married-couple families were living in poverty, compared to 44 percent of children in mother-only families.[11]

- A study of juvenile offenders indicated that family structure significantly predicts delinquency.[12]

- Single parenthood ratios were strongly correlated with violent crimes.[13]

- Children with more involved fathers experienced fewer behavioral problems and scored higher on reading achievement.[14]

The above data is a small sample of the impact of fatherlessness on children. These facts are seen daily in the media. Many boys will never reach manhood based on these statistics, and those who do reach adulthood are scarred. These scars influence their ability to lead themselves, to lead their families, and even to become leaders in the church one day.

The Bible addresses the fathers' roles in the development of their children. According to Ephesians 6:4 Paul states "ye fathers, provoke not your children to wrath: but bring them up in the nurture and admonition of the Lord." This means Fathers are called to correct their children. Fathers are to have loving concern for their children. Fathers are to encourage their children in self-control. Fathers are to instruct their children in the Lord.

The parable of the prodigal son told by Jesus in Luke chapter 15 is an example a father helping his sons achieves "True Manhood." The father had previously taught his sons the true concept of manhood. The younger son leaves his father and makes numerous mistakes; however, it is the father's love and teaching that helps the son find his way back home. The father receives the younger son back. He also teaches the older son the virtue of forgiveness.

These lessons of how fathers are to treat their children are invaluable in helping boys become men. These are also characteristic that are needed for those who will become leaders in the Lord's church.

Leadership Candidates

We began this study with a series of questions with regards to having men with leadership qualities and desires. We have looked at the changes in society, the effect of work habits on both the quantity and quality of family time especially that of fathers and sons. The concept of "True Manhood" was defined both legally and biblically. The concept of God's requirement for men to become committed in their relationships is preparing them for other leadership roles were also explored. Additionally, the effects of both physical and emotional fatherlessness are highlighted; these being viable factors in the transformation from being a boy to becoming a man.

Let us now consider the biblical qualification for leadership. Paul writes in his 1ˢᵗ letter to Timothy in the third chapter concerning bishops, their qualifications and work, 1-7; of deacons, and how they should be proved, 8-10; and of their wives and children, and how they should be governed, 11-13.

This is a true saying, if a man desires the office of a bishop, he desireth a good work. A bishop then must be blameless, the husband of one wife, vigilant, sober, of good behaviour, given to hospitality, apt to teach; Not given to wine, no striker, not greedy of filthy lucre; but patient, not a brawler, not covetous; One that ruleth well his own house, having his children in subjection with all gravity; (For if a man know not how to rule his own house, how shall he take care of the church of God?) Not a novice, lest being lifted up with pride he fall into the condemnation of the devil. Moreover he must have a good report of them which are without; lest he fall into reproach and the snare of the devil. Likewise must the deacons be grave, not double-tongued, not given to much wine, not greedy of filthy lucre; Holding the mystery of the faith in a pure conscience. And let these also first be proved; then let them use the office of a deacon, being found blameless. Even so must their wives be grave, not slanderers, sober, faithful in all things. Let the deacons be the husbands of one wife, ruling their children and their own houses well. For they that have used the office of a deacon well purchase to themselves a good degree, and great boldness in the faith which is in Christ Jesus (1 Timothy 3:1-13).

These biblical qualifications for leadership that Paul shares with Timothy do align with the concept of boys becoming men. I have severed as a minister in the Lord's church for over twenty-years; my brother is serving as a deacon at his local church. I credit our leadership in our families, the community, and the church to our father who is also a minister. Our father has helped us to transition from boyhood to manhood.

Can we in the church have a pool of qualified men who are ready for leadership? Yes. Can we develop faithful men who are committed to the word of God that will teach others as well? Yes. Can we help men develop a desire to become leaders in the church? Yes, we can but it will start with helping our boys to become true Men.

Biography

1. Justice, Extent, Nature, and Consequences of Intimate Partner Violence, July 2000. The Commonwealth Fund, Health Concerns Across a Woman's Lifespan: 1998 Survey of Women's Health, 1999

2. (Bureau of Justice Statistics Crime Data Brief, Intimate Partner Violence, 1993-2001, February 2003)

3. Bureau of Justice Statistics, Violence Against Women: Estimates from the Redesigned Survey, August 1995

4. (Bureau of Justice Statistics, Intimate Partner Violence in the U.S. 1993-2004, 2006.)

5. Allstate Foundation National Poll on Domestic Violence, 2006

6. Bureau of Justice Statistics Crime Data Brief, Intimate Partner Violence, 1993-2001

7. Jay G. Silverman, PhD; Anita Raj, PhD; Lorelei A. Mucci, MPH; and Jeanne E. Hathaway, MD, MPH, "Dating Violence Against Adolescent Girls and Associated Substance Use, Unhealthy Weight Control, Sexual Risk Behavior, Pregnancy, and Suicidality," Journal of the American Medical Association, Vol. 286, No. 5, 2001

8. Information provided by Oregon Law Center

9. National Center for Fathering, Fathering in America Poll, January, 1999.

10. Krieder, Rose M. and Jason Fields. Living Arrangements of Children 2001. Current Population Reports, p. 70-104. Table 1. Washington, DC: U.S. Census Bureau, 2005.

11. U.S. Census Bureau, Children's Living Arrangements and Characteristics: March 2011, Table C8. Washington D.C.: 2011.

12. Bush, Connee, Ronald L. Mullis, and Ann K. Mullis. "Differences in Empathy Between Offender and Nonoffender Youth." Journal of Youth and Adolescence 29 (August 2000): 467-478.

13. Barber, Nigel. "Single Parenthood As a Predictor of Cross-National Variation in Violent Crime." Cross-Cultural Research 38 (November 2004): 343-358.
14. Howard, K. S., Burke Lefever, J. E., Borkowski, J.G., & Whitman , T. L. (2006). Fathers' influence in the lives of children with adolescent mothers. Journal of Family Psychology, 20, 468- 476.

Herman E. Wesley III

Herman E. Wesley III is the minister of the NorthPointe Church of Christ in Montgomery, Alabama and is the CEO of the Herman Wesley Companies USA and Publishing Founder of *The Revivalist Newsmagazine, Contemporary Christian Woman Magazine* and therevivalist.com. A graduate of Southwestern Christian College and Oklahoma Christian University, he was the recipient of an Honorary Doctorate of Ministry from the National Academy of Christian Studies in Fort Worth, Texas in 2010 and named to the Southwestern Christian College Alumni Hall of Fame. He also serves on the Advisory Board of the National Lectureship and hosts the CORNERSTONE CONFERENCE annually in Montgomery, Alabama.

Originally from Newark, New Jersey he was mentored by the legendary Dr. Eugene Lawton. He is married to Sonja for thirty years and is the father of two sons, Brandon JeMarcus and Christian Rischard.

CHAPTER 14

Fractionalization

Dr. Herman E. Wesley III

—◦◦◦—

frac·tion·al·ize [**frak**-shu*h*-nl-ahyz]

verb (used with object), verb (used without object),
frac·tion·al·ized, frac·tion·al·iz·ing.

to divide or splinter into fractions, sections, factions, etc.

*"...the sentence structure is the same, worded, basically, the same way: In **Acts 20:7** and in **I Corinthians 16:2**, the Bible says, "upon the first day of the week!" If "first day of the week means every week when it comes to the money, then it ought to mean the first day of every week when it comes to communion, because it's worded the same way..."*

I was in a gospel meeting in Santa Monica, California with Minister O.J. Dyson, working the chalkboard and making my point, vigorously, when I realized how absolutely wrong I was. I remember thinking, "You better hope nobody is here who will challenge you on this statement, because you know it's wrong." I was relieved when no one challenged me, but I was mentally shaken. Growing up in the church, and being exposed to many legendary preachers of the Gospel in the bosom of the Newark Church, I, along with many people across the country, heard this illustration often, preached with conviction and surety. It was foundational. Bedrock. It was that which becometh "sound doctrine." Yet, standing alone, contextually, as an argument, it was faulty. Now, you can be certain that the mere mention of this discrepancy will be viewed, by some, as heretical, non-conformist and apostate.

That is precisely the problem.

Preaching and teaching with integrity is at my core, even through my struggles. As I seek to rise above personal challenges, my teaching needs to be solid and sound, and on this occasion, I failed. As a means of explanation, it is abundantly clear that the directive in **Acts 20:7** is not the same as the directive in **I Corinthians 16:2**. While **Acts 20:7** speaks to the common and consistent practice of the early church gathering on the first day of every week, the context and situation of **I Corinthians 16:2** is a one-time benevolent offering being gathered for the distresses and poverty of Christians in Judea, which, at this time, were extraordinary, partly through general calamities of that nation, and partly through the particular sufferings to which they were exposed. While I do believe the early church established a pattern of first day of the week giving, this scripture speaks to a specific, free will offering, for a specific purpose.

I personally believe that one of the major challenges that will confront the churches of Christ over the next few years, black congregations in particular, will be, what I term fractionalization. This is an issue as old as the church itself, this inward pull to divide or splinter into fractions, factions and sections. This issue is woven throughout the early church, as witnessed in the incessant work of the Judaizers as seen in the letter to the **Galatians**, and in the divisive nature of the church at Corinth, which Paul addressed in **I Corinthians chapter 1**.

In this article, we will explore some historical influences and their impact on our brotherhood, and factors that contribute to this subject. It is also very important for me to note that while we have had historically significant institutions, there are many Schools of Preaching, Christian Colleges and regional lectureships and platforms that have contributed positively to the comprehensive history of the contemporary church. There have also been great and notable ministers who have had significant impact on the church, outside of the stream of our traditional institutions. This article is not designed to diminish or degrade any of these contributions.

There are a number of current events that have and will continue to bring fractionalization to the forefront:

THE QUEST FOR BIBLICAL INTEGRITY

In that Gospel Meeting in Santa Monica, I was hit with the reality of how important it is for each minister or teacher of the Gospel to not only preach that of which they are convicted, but to make sure that conviction is sound. We cannot and should not parrot what we have heard over the years without studying it for ourselves. At this moment, my own personal study subliminally attacked my public teaching, and I was embarrassed. Each generation must study anew our accepted teachings to reach our own personal conclusions and convictions. As our teachings are reviewed and studied, and as different conclusions may be reached on a variety of issues that differ from traditionally accepted conclusions, fractionalization will occur. The challenge, then, will be our acceptance or rejection of new conclusions, and since we have no formal hierarchal structure, those who reach similar conclusions will begin to gravitate to each other, forming a variety of "association fellowships" that will tear at the semblance of unity we've enjoyed for the past forty years. New approaches and, in some cases, an enlightened study of the scriptures, are often met with skepticism. This skepticism can become debilitating and off putting as men are labeled "change agents." This is unfortunate.

It is because of the undying dedication and commitment of our forebears that a great number of our young and new preachers are afforded an opportunity to reach deeper into some commonly used texts, and, through a study of original language and relevant, period specific customs **(See Romans 16:16)**, share this education with an increasingly hungry, thirsty and research enabled membership.

Unfortunately, because of these changes, we are failing to recognize a clear, biblical dynamic that reveals the fact that congregations grow and mature at different paces. Because we have no national structure or organization, each congregation moves as it deems appropriate relative to their own understanding of scripture under what we call an "autonomous" leadership, which Webster defines as: *existing or acting separately from other things or people.: having the power or right to govern itself.*

This is significant, because where, at one time, there was uniformity to most practices in various congregations across the nation, that is not the norm now. Consequently, we must be cautious to not allow judgmentalism to infiltrate and infect our fellowship **(Romans 14)**. We must be very careful, moving forward, to not marginalize or ostracize those ministers and ministries that move beyond the borders of our familiarity and comfort. There must be an honest discussion and understanding as to what is traditional and what is scriptural; what is detrimental to scriptural fellowship, and what is allowed in Christian liberty; that "different" is not the same thing as "wrong" **(see Acts 16:1-3)**.

There are doctrinal positions and teachings that are distinctive and unique to the church of the New Testament; our belief in the virgin birth of Christ. Our belief that Christ is the fulfillment of the Messianic prophecies, and that He is God in the flesh. Our understanding that salvation emanates from our obedience to the message and mission of Christ; His prophecy **(Matthew 16:13-18; Luke 24:43-52)**, substantiated by Old Testament prophecies **(Isaiah 2:2; Zechariah 1:16; Daniel 2:44)**, concerning His church, and the oneness of it **(Ephesians 4:1-4)**; His vicarious death on the cross and His resurrection from the dead **(I Corinthians 15:3-4)**, now being seated on the right hand of God **(Ephesians 1:19-23)**; and the universal requirement of belief **(Romans 10:17)**, repentance **(Acts 17:30)**, confession **(Romans 10:10)** and baptism **(Matthew 28:19; Acts 8:36-38)**, by immersion **(Romans 6:1-4; Colossians 2:12)**, for the remission of sins and the reception of God's Holy Spirit **(Acts 2:38)**; our steadfast commitment to the apostles' doctrine **(Acts 2:41)**.

THE DECLINE OF INSTITUTIONAL LOYALTY

The unity we've enjoyed in the past was related to the singleness of institutions and the overarching influence of a small number of strong-willed, visionary preachers. The tremendous work of G.P. Bowser and Marshall Keeble, and their boy preachers who were mentored by them and traveled with them provided our brotherhood with solid leadership and practical wisdom. Through relationship ties from Nashville Christian Institute and Silver Point Bible Institute, loyalties were formed amongst the "Keeble boys" and the "Bowser boys," culminating in the development of the National Lectureship and Southwestern Christian College. Additionally, the founding and distribution of The Christian Echo served as a tool to unite thought and speech and give credible foundation to issues and doctrinal teaching, mirroring the influence of thought and dialogue of The Gospel Advocate among the white brethren. These institutions flourished during a period when Blacks in the churches of Christ were marginalized and operated under a segregated system. There were lectureships held among white members, but we were not generally invited to attend or participate. Many of the Christian colleges associated with the Church of Christ were not open to Blacks attending. It has been noted that Abilene Christian University in Abilene, Texas was the last private educational institution of higher learning in the State of Texas to allow Blacks admission. During this era, there was a great movement among Blacks which led to the birth of the National Lectureship, first being held in Oklahoma City at the Seventh Street Church of Christ in March 1945, and Southwestern Christian College in Terrell, Texas in 1948. These two bedrock institutions, along with The Christian Echo, founded by G.P. Bowser in 1902, served as clearinghouses for doctrinal teaching, introducing and reducing ministers, elevating and leveling ministers, (whether intended or unintended) and relationship building that has extended itself even to this day.

However, because of societal changes, the proliferation of Christian Schools, and the opening of opportunities for admission into these schools, the cohesiveness that was characteristic of the Black church has waned. The great majority of pulpits across the nation, at one time, were occupied by graduates of Southwestern Christian College, or supporters of the school. That has changed dramatically. Just as, in the Old Testament, a generation arose that knew not the Lord, nor yet the works which He had done for Israel (**Judges 2:10**), this generation, while they know the Lord, are far removed from the struggles and victories of the post-restoration movement of Blacks in the Lord's Church throughout the fifties, sixties and early seventies. Mirroring society, the support and allegiance to those institutions that once thrived are dying, and there is no resurgence of effort to keep them alive. This is, partly, because these institutions have failed to adapt and remain relevant for new generations. Generational shifts have been, for the most part, ignored, and our institutions are suffering because of it. I recommend "One Church: Four Generations" by Gary L. McIntosh. In this book he shares how societal impacts have shaped generational responses, and he gives great insight as to how these various generations can be reached by tailoring ministries and outreach to specifically meet these generational needs. One generation has a steadfast sense of loyalty, and do as they are instructed, without showing weakness through emotions; another generation has to ask "why," and readily questions authority, is prone to emotional swings, but once they are convinced, become great contributors to a congregation. These two groups (actually five) exist in the average congregation today, and there is a tension beneath the surface that, oftentimes, manifests itself in congregational splits, not out of hatred or anger, but out of a sense of feeling like an outsider because *that sister who was placed over the kitchen in 1962 is still there, and I cannot work with her because she thinks I'm trying to replace her!"*

THE FAILURE OF PROGRESSIVE MENTORSHIP

Moses mentored Joshua. Elijah mentored Elisha. Paul mentored Timothy and Titus. Bowser mentored through Silver Point Bible Institute. Keeble mentored through Nashville Christian Institute. Hogan, Winston, Steward, Kennedy mentored our senior generation above us, but the succeeding generations have not been as generous in their mentorship. For the most part, this is where our mentoring process begins to break down. It is supremely important to peer into the dynamics of these mentoring relationships in order to understand the loyalties and continuities of brotherhood cohesiveness and respect.

We have witnessed the breakdown of the African-American family, and can give a cacophony of reasons to explain this disintegration. What we must also recognize is that the same reasons which explain the breakdown of the African-American family tend to be the same reasons we have had a breakdown, or fracture, in the church. The lack of strong, consistent male leadership; the absence of men in the church; the failure of men in the church to adhere to Paul's instruction to the young preacher Titus in **Titus chapter 2**

207

and verse 2, and the failure of our senior men to develop honest, non-judgmental, instructional and positive reinforcing relationships with younger men.

From my own personal experience, it is the connection I have with Dr. Eugene Lawton that keeps me focused and grounded. Not perfect...but grounded. While I may have lost things, I have never lost my faith! I have witnessed many preachers in my generation fall away, even mounting denominational pulpits on a full-time basis, because they have no "mentor roots" in the church. Much time has been spent honing the craft (of preaching) as opposed to embracing the Spirit. Joshua walked with Moses, Elisha walked with Elijah, Titus and Timothy walked with Paul, and, I believe, Paul had intimate knowledge of their life, their development, their background and influences **(2 Timothy 1:5)**. This becomes so important in ministerial development because it fosters continuity. As these mentors walked before their students, their weaknesses and strengths were exposed; however, it is through this authentic and transparent walk that the glory of God is witnessed as it is manifested in the work of the Lord. Moses disobeyed God, Paul was somewhat duplicitous in the circumcision scenario, but these incidences in no way were the sum total of these Spirit-filled lives which led God's people through the Old Testament, and, through the writings of Paul, continue to lead God's people today.

This connection is vitally important, because without it many new and young preachers feel as if they do not matter, and they are all alone. While each individual must be secure in his or her own relationship and walk with Christ, it cannot be denied that having a mentor is beneficial during times of struggle, ambivalence and spiritual introspection. Mentorship, however, cannot be coerced or imposed. It comes by process of selection, and this can only come through relationship. Many seasoned, mature preachers like to claim "Fathership" with an increasing number of young and new ministers, based on a false rubric: A young man may have grown into manhood in our city or a particular region of the country. "Sonship," however, is not inherent in our proximity to older preachers, meaning that because we grow up in the shadows of older or mature ministers we are not automatically mentored by them. "Sonship" is borne out of "relationship," which requires more than passive association. It involves intimate and consistent interaction. Passive association and mentorship are not the same thing.

In mentoring relationships, it is important that a safe zone be established where honest and open dialogue can take place without the fear of being labeled or categorized. True study will always birth questions about the faith and doctrine, and we are only made stronger when we can have that discussion in a non-threatening environment. There are many preachers in our succeeding generations that are striving to be true to biblical context, and, in the process, are questioning many positions that have been historically held by the church at large. It is not the questions that should be our cause of concern, but our hesitancy to deal with them in a mature manner, ensuring that respect for the Word is held in the highest esteem over respect for institution. Just as with the U.S. Constitution, the Bible is a living document and the church is a living institution, which means that while all truth has been revealed and is complete, our understanding and implementation is still maturing. Even with the church, while Christ said, "I will build," in **Matthew 16:18**, Paul has us to know that WE are laborers together with God in this process **(I Corinthians 3:5-11)**. It becomes, then, a joint venture, where Christ is the Contractor and we are the subcontractor, with the expectation that we will build according to the specifications of Christ. It is an ongoing, daily process.

There must also be accessibility and, what I call, touchability, from older and more mature church leaders and preachers to the young, developing searcher. It requires a dropping of the guard on both parts, and a sense of vulnerability, on both parts as well.

CONCLUSION

In **I Corinthians 1:10 (NKJV)** we see the instruction,

"Now I plead with you, brethren, by the name of our Lord Jesus Christ, that you all speak the same thing, and that there be no divisions among you, but that you be perfectly joined together in the same mind and in the same judgment."

And while we have always taken this as a "brotherhood" instruction, contextually, it was a congregational instruction. We are hard pressed to find two congregations across the nation that speak "the same thing" on every issue. Truth is, we are hard pressed to find that in any city! The point is that a single congregation must be on the same page, moving the same way, as to protect congregational unity. The Lord's Church, universally, must be united, but as we have mentioned earlier, we are all not at the same level of maturity **(Hebrews 5:12)**. The admonition of Paul to the church at Rome would do well for us, if we are to avoid fractionalization:

Romans 14:17-20 (NKJV):

"for the kingdom of God is not eating and drinking, but righteousness and peace and joy in the Holy Spirit. For he who serves Christ in these things is acceptable to God and approved by men. Therefore let us pursue the things which make for peace and the things by which one may edify another. Do not destroy the work of God for the sake of food. All things indeed are pure, but it is evil for the man who eats with offense."

We are going to have to walk in maturity, brethren. We must know when doctrine is being challenged or diminished, and we must have discernment to determine if it is an area of liberty. We must contend the faith **(Jude 1:3)**, but we must also love the brotherhood **(I Peter 2:17)**. My prayer is that we will have the wisdom to know the difference. If we fail to heed this instruction, each man will retreat to his own corner, with his own friends, and the body will downward spiral into fractions, and this, dear friends, is contrary to the Spirit and Will of our God.

CHAPTER 15

Passionate Pleadings That Prepare Us for the Future

John Davis Marshall

—⁓—

The Holy Spirit guided the writer John to write with purpose. He included the record of signs that Jesus performed so as to cause people to believe that Jesus is the Christ, the Son of God; and that believing they might have life in His name (John 20:30). Though John's record is not exhaustive, it is adequate to accomplish God's intended purpose (John 21:25). We therefore, expect our studying of the stories to advance our faith.

Interaction, The Faith Developer

John chapter 4 contains a record of some whose faith was developed and advanced. Therein, Jesus interacted with three categories of people: the Samaritan woman, the Samaritan men, and the royal official (John 4:1-54). He attempted to strengthen their faith. In each instance, their faith became stronger.

213

How great is your faith? How great do you want your faith to be? Your faith can be as great as you are willing to make it.

Initially, we start with a recommended faith. Initially, they believed because of what others had recommended. Because of recommendation, the woman believed (John 4:19-20; 25). Because of recommendation, the men believed (John 4:39, 28-30). Because of recommendation, the royal official believed (John 4:46-47).

Subsequently, we progress to a verified faith. Subsequently, they believed because of what they had verified. Because of verification, the woman believed (John 4:16-19, 28-29). Because of verification, the men believed (John 4:39-42). Because of verification, the official believed (John 4:49-53).

Your faith can be as great as you would like it to be. Faithful interaction with people of faith moves your faith from recommendation to verification. The woman interacted with Jesus who was a person of faith, the men interacted with the woman who was a person of faith, and the official interacted with others of faith.

Only through faithful participation can you verify your faith. Jesus invites us to "come see" (John 1:39). God invited people to trust Him (Malachi 3:10).

Your faith can be as great as you want it to be. Interaction is the great faith developer. Your faith can be as great as you are willing to interact with people of faith. Men had interacted with the woman before [she had had five husbands] she became a woman of faith and their interaction did nothing to progress their faith.

Let's examine a slice of the story and see how Jesus impacted faith. Traveling from Judea to Galilee, Jesus went through Samaria (John 4:3-4). Samaria sat on the west side of the Jordan River sandwiched between Galilee to the north and Judea to the south. Traveling through Samaria seemed to have been of geographical necessity.

However, the Jews had traditionally avoided going through Samaria by crossing over to the east side of the Jordan River, passing by Samaria, and then crossing back to the west side of the Jordan River. Therefore, it was not of geographical necessity that Jesus would pass through Samaria. It was of social and theological necessity that He would pass through Samaria.

The Sociological Road Least Traveled

Jesus traveled the social road that was least traveled. Sometimes, God expects us to walk the social road that is least traveled. When we walk the social road that is least traveled good things happen. When we walk the social road that is least traveled, we bring social harmony between different culture groups. What a good thing that should happen?

In 722 B. C., the Assyrians captured the 10 Northern tribes of Israel and deported the healthy men to Mesopotamia (2 Kings 17:6-41). Foreigners migrated into the formerly Jewish occupied territory and married the Jewish women who remained. The descendants from this cohabitation became known as Samaritans, half-breeds. In 536 B. C., Zerubbabel led the first Jewish return from Babylonian exile to Jerusalem to rebuild the city. Imagine that. What do you think happened when the Jewish men returned to Jerusalem and discovered that Gentile men had married Jewish women? What do you think happened when the heritage exclusive Jews discovered that Jerusalem was now occupied by half-breeds? What had once been so precious to them was now in the control of Gentiles. The war was on. Irritation, agitation, and frustration ensued. From that time the social divide invaded their ranks (Ezra 4:1-3).

By the time of Jesus, the Jews had avoided socially interacting with the Samaritans for more than 500 years. The Jews had continually refused to socially interact with the Samaritans (John 4:9). It is no wonder that the woman at the well was surprised that Jesus would ask her for a drink.

However, the Jews did economically interact with the Samaritans. Remember that the disciples had gone into the city to buy food (John 4:8).

Jesus socialized with a Samaritan. He socialized with a Samaritan woman. He asked the woman for a drink of water. He had nothing from which to draw water and drink. Therefore, He must then have been willing to drink water from her cup, put his lips where her lips had been. Only those who are family, socially close, will drink from the same container as another. Jesus was willing to treat this woman as if she family.

When we walk the social road that is least traveled, we bring social harmony between the gender groups. What a good thing to happen.

Jesus publically socialized with a Samaritan woman (John 4:7). We bring social harmony between the gender groups. Jewish men avoided socializing publicly with women (John 4:27). When His disciples saw Him talking with a woman, it was so far from the norm, they just remained silent. When behavior deviates slightly from the norm, we ask questions. When behavior deviates greatly from the norm, we as shocked into silence. For example, if I enter the room with my shirt on backwards, everyone will say, "What are you doing?" But if I enter the room with my pants on my arms and my shirt on my legs, you are likely to look at me and wonder in silence.

God expects us to walk the social road that is least traveled. Gender strife, the battle between the sexes proves that males and females need to learn better how to respond to each other.

Strife, between the male and female, creeps through the cracks of misguided cultural traditions. Because of misguided cultural traditions created by men, the disciples of Christ had to learn how to respond to women. They were amazed that Jesus being a man would publicly talk with a woman (John 4:27).

Jesus who is the sociological light of the world did not restrict Himself to the misguided cultural traditions of His day. He is the light, who when followed, will minimize gender strife. We may safely follow Him. We ought never restrict nor be restricted to the misguided cultural traditions of our day.

Strife, between the male and female, seeps through the seams of misapplied scriptural traditions. Because of misapplied scriptural traditions the scribes and Pharisees, who were religious zealots, had to learn how to respond to women. They brought a woman who had been taken in the very act of adultery; yet, they had neglected [likely intentional] to bring the man (John 8:3-11). The Law called for the stoning of both (Leviticus 20:10, Deuteronomy 22:22). Where was the man?

Down through the centuries males have misused the scriptures to abuse and abandon females (Matthew 19:3-8). Recently, I read an article arguing that a man could divorce his wife but that a wife could not divorce her husband. How sad that any divorce is needed to be exercised. It is even sadder to argue for one against the other.

Even now, unmarried females who become pregnant are often banished from sight. At best, their church participation is marginalized at least during their pregnancy. We attempt to justify our treatment by claiming that they will negatively influence the other young girls.

When does she cease to negatively influence? Folk will always remember that she gave birth to a child out of wedlock. How will the mother ever be able to participate in the body life of the church? When will the mother ever be able to participate in the body life of the church? Likely, only after a group of men, controlled by their wives, vouch her back into faithfulness. How sad.

The girls did not produce the babies by themselves. Where are the males? Often while the females are banished the males gain notoriety.

When a believer has acknowledged and repented of sin, what sound scriptural basis do we have for restricting their activities within the body life of the church (Luke 15:19-24)? That was the crippling attitude of the older brother.

Jesus who is the sociological light of the world did not restrict Himself to the misapplied scriptural traditions of His day. We may safely follow Him. We ought never restrict nor be restricted to the misapplied scriptural traditions of our day.

The Theological Road Least Traveled

Jesus walked the theological road that was least traveled. Sometimes, God expects us to walk the theological (worship) road that is least traveled. When we walk the theological road that is least traveled good things happen.

When we walk the theological road that is least traveled, we create the opportunity to remove ignorance that leads to false worship. What a good thing to happen.

God set His name in Jerusalem for the worship place (Deuteronomy 16:2, 5-6, 11; 1 Kings 5:2-5, 9:1-3, 2 Kings 18:22, 2 Kings 23:21-23, Luke 2:41, John 2:13, 23).

The Samaritans moved the place of worship from Jerusalem (2 Kings 17:6, 24-33, Ezra 4:1-24, Nehemiah 4:1-3). Therefore, the Samaritan woman ignorantly participated in a contaminated worship (John 4:22). Her ancestors had ignorantly participated in a contaminated worship (2 Kings 17:24-41). Even before them, king Jeroboam had caused Israel to sin (1 Kings 15:25-26; 30; 33-34; 1 Kings 14:14-16).

King Jeroboam changed the *place* of the worship (1 Kings 12:25-30, Deuteronomy 16:2, 5-6, 11; 1 Kings 5:2-5, 9:1-3,

2 Kings 18:22, 2 Kings 23:21-23, Luke 2:41, John 2:13, 23). God had said that Jerusalem is the place, but Jeroboam said that he would decide. Therefore, he set up a golden calf in Dan and one in Bethel for them to behold as their gods.

King Jeroboam changed the *priests* (the people who led the worship) of the worship (1 Kings 12:31, 13:33-34). Only those of the tribe of Levi could serve as priests (Numbers 1:49-50). Jeroboam decided to make priest from those other than the tribe of Levi.

King Jeroboam he changed the *period* of the worship (1 Kings 12:32-33; Leviticus 23:4-6; 15-37, Deuteronomy 16:16, 2 Chronicles 8:13). God decreed that the first month on the fourteenth day of the month the Passover would be celebrated. Jeroboam decided that the eighth month and the fifteenth day was acceptable.

When we walk the theological road that is least traveled, we create the opportunity to implant knowledge that leads to true worship. What a good thing to happen.

True worshippers will worship the Father. The Father seeks true worshippers to worship Him. Who are the true worshippers?

True worshippers know the God they worship. Jesus reminded her that salvation was from the Jews (John 4:22b). True worshippers are those who have been made holy, for worship is an activity of the redeemed.

True worshippers worship the God they know. Jesus reminded her of their ignorance in worship (John 4:22a). Too often those who seek to worship are ignorant of the God they seek to worship (2 Kings 17:26-29, Acts 17:22-23).

True worshippers will worship the Father in spirit and truth. The Father seeks true worshippers, who will worship Him in spirit and truth. What does that mean?

True worshippers worship the Father in spirit. Jesus reminded the woman that worship would no longer be confined to a physical place (John 4:21). God is spirit and therefore to worship in spirit is to be in God not limited to a physical place (John 4:24, Acts 17:24-28; 7:48-50).

True worshippers worship the Father in spirit and in truth. Jesus reminded the woman that truth must be known (John 4:22) Jesus is the truth. Therefore, those who worship in truth must first be in Jesus (John 14:6, 5:32-36).

God expects us to walk the worship road that is least traveled. Worship is a holy experience. Therefore, God is the only One whom you must seek to please. You do not automatically know how to engage properly in the holy experience of worship. You must learn how to reverently engage in the holy experience of worship (2 Kings 17:28). You struggle to abandon traditional worship practices. All worship is not acceptable. Some worship is unacceptable (2 kings 17:24-41, Matthew 15:8-9).

Some, who are outside of the body of Christ, worship ignorantly. They care, but know not how to worship Him. Some, who are within the body of Christ, worship negligently. They know, but care not how they worship Him. God desires for all to be in the body of Christ and worship Him intentionally and knowledgeably.

For too long we have crossed the river of political correctness, passed by the Samaria of social and theological transformation, and left the hearts of God's people unchallenged and unchanged.

Like the gospel of John, **Church Matters** is written with purpose. **Church Matters** is of moral necessity. **Church Matters** will seek to lead you into a faithful interaction with those who are seeking to be faithful to Jesus. **Church Matters** will seek to lead you along the sociological road that is least traveled. **Church Matters** will seek to lead you along the theological road that is leas traveled. If then we can succeed, we will both improve the health of our faith.

CPSIA information can be obtained at www.ICGtesting.com
Printed in the USA
LVOW12*0312050314

376064LV00003B/4/P